MAKING SENSE OF EARLY LITERACY:

Le A PRACTITIONER'S PERSPECTIVE

STANDARD LOAN

UNLESS RECALLED BY ANOTHER READER
THIS ITEM MAY BE BORROWED FOR

FOUR WEEKS

To renew, online at: http://prism.talis.com/chi-ac/
or by telephone: 01243 816089 (Bishop Otter)
01243 812099 (Bognor Regis)

MAKING SENSE OF EARLY LITERACY:
A PRACTITIONER'S PERSPECTIVE

Tricia David, Bridie Raban, Christine Ure,
Kathy Goouch, Martine Jago, Isabelle Barrière
and Andrew Lambirth

Trentham Books

Stoke on Trent, UK and Sterling, USA

Trentham Books Limited

Westview House   22883 Quicksilver Drive
734 London Road   Sterling
Oakhill   VA 20166-2012
Stoke on Trent   USA
Staffordshire
England ST4 5NP

First published 2000

British Library Cataloguing-in-Publication Data
A catalogue record for this book is available from the British Library

1 85856 223 6 (paperback)

Designed and typeset by Trentham Print Design Ltd., Chester and printed in Great Britain by Cromwell Press Ltd., Wiltshire.

Contents

Preface and acknowledgements

The research and development projects upon which the contents of this book are based have been conducted in four countries: Australia (with its many different states and thus education systems), England (with its increasingly centralised control of the curriculum for children in schools and nurseries funded by the government), France (where there is more than a hundred years of nursery provision, each citizen's entitlement), and Singapore (a multilingual, high achieving society). The authors of the two early literacy projects, one based at the University of Melbourne, Australia, the other at Canterbury Christ Church University College, England, have collaborated not only by crossing state boundaries and meeting up with each other and with a great many educators in different countries; e-mail (in other words, print – 'writing' created by team members) has been a key mode of communication.

In their attempts to make sense of the ways in which different countries, different societies, and within them different stakeholders hold differing views about young children's learning and, in particular, what it is appropriate to expect of children before they enter elementary/primary education, the team members have had many real and virtual discussions and there are still some aspects on which they continue to strive for shared understanding. This is not surprising, however, since jointly, the teams' backgrounds represent an exciting professional and academic mix from the disciplines and fields of: linguistics, psycholinguistics, psychology, language and literacy, early childhood education, human biology, educational research and policy. Nevertheless, they are in total agreement that children born into print-dependent societies will seek to make sense of their worlds – worlds that also include print. The children will be shaped by these worlds – and, in their turn, seek to shape them too, given the opportunity.

Both teams owe numerous debts of gratitude: to colleagues in the field of Early Childhood Education in the four countries; to the Esmée Fairbairn Charitable Trust for funding the Early Literacy Links project at Canterbury Christ Church University College; to the University of Melbourne for funding work in Australia and Singapore; to Louise Duff, Annie McLaren and Roma Woodward for secretarial support; and to the Trentham Books team for their patience and publishing expertise.

As authors we would also like to acknowledge gratitude to our partners, families and friends, and in particular to the early years teachers and children with whom we have all been priviledged to work: Dr. M. Lorch, Dr. I. Sinka, J. Tyson, S. Khazara, S. Radulovic and all the active members of Mangobajito café for their essential contributions to Isabelle's work; Jacinta and Benson for being Christine's teachers in life; all the participants in Martine's doctoral study; the children at Bellwood Nursery and their remarkable teacher Jeanette for allowing Kathy to listen to their stories; the children and schools Andrew has been privileged to work with and the colleagues who support him; Carley, Tara and Lily for providing Bridie with astounding pleasure, as they gain control of the print-rich environment that surrounds them; and Coralie, Eliot and Kieran for the hundreds of everyday examples of young children's brilliance, with which they enhance Tricia's ability to 'make sense' of early learning.

Canterbury and Melbourne April 2000

About the authors

Christine Ure is Associate Dean for Preservice Programmes at the University of Melbourne and previously coordinated the Bachelor of Early Childhood Studies in Melbourne and Singapore. Christine's research interest involves issues concerning educational provision for children in preschool and the early years of schooling. She is particularly interested in factors that influence teachers' expectations for children and how these impact on continuity in curriculum provision as children move from preschool to school.

Kathy Goouch is a Senior Lecturer at Canterbury Christ Church University College. She has enjoyed a range of teaching experience in schools in London and Kent. Her interest in young children's literacy has developed over many years and her research focus is in young children's ability to construct meaning through reading and mark making. Kathy is currently enjoying listening to children learning in nurseries.

Isabelle Barrière is a Lecturer in Linguistics and Developmental Psycholinguistics at the University of Hertfordshire. Her research interests lie in the cross-linguistic study of language acquisition, literacy, the psycholinguistic aspects of bilingualism (including code-switching and bi-modal communication) and the educational and clinical applications of psycholinguistic investigations.

Bridie Raban holds the Mooroolbeek Foundation Chair of Early Childhood at the University of Melbourne, Australia. Bridie's research is focused on children's language and literacy development, and on teacher development and change. During 1999 and 2000 she has been the first research fellow seconded to the Department of Education, Training and Youth Affairs, where she has worked in the area of policy and research for the government of the Commonwealth of Australia.

Martine Jago has an MA in Modern Foreign Languages from St Anne's College, Oxford. Until 1995 she was a deputy headteacher of a primary and nursery school in Hertfordshire and subsequently a full-time doctoral student, researching foreign languages in early schooling, until taking up her post as a member of the Early Literacy Links research team. Martine is currently a Senior Lecturer in the Faculty of Education at Canterbury Christ Church University College.

Andrew Lambirth is currently a Senior Lecturer in Education at Canterbury Christ Church University College. Andrew taught in London primary schools before joining higher education. He has particular interests in the area of children's literacy development, poetry and children's literature. Andrew's publications are concerned with the teaching of poetry in primary schools.

Tricia David is a Professor of Education at Canterbury, where she is currently Head of the Centre for Educational Research. Tricia's early childhood research experience spans over a quarter of a century, having begun in the early 1970s and having continued during the many years when she was a nursery and primary school teacher and headteacher. She has always found much to be learned by 'crossing boundaries' in her search for understanding – boundaries between disciplines, countries, services and government departments.

1

Early literacy in a fast-changing world

New millennium, new world

At the opening of the new millennium, life in advanced industrial and post-industrial societies such as Australia, England, France and Singapore seems to move at an ever increasing pace. Information enters our homes via media our grandparents would never have dreamt of. In an instant we can contact friends on the other side of the world. We can shop for 24 hours seven days a week. Many children grow up without experiencing the rhythms and cyclical patterns of nature and the production of food, which were for so long an everyday part of community survival. Large numbers of babies and children live far from their extended families. Some have parents who manage to form surrogate extended families with friends and neighbours, or through taking their children to nurseries or childminders. The period in which we are now living may be one in which the fastest changes (apart from those caused by wars) are occurring in the way people live.

Young children are eminently adaptable but they usually like what is familiar to them and new experiences embedded in the familiar are likely to provide the most appropriate challenges from which young children can learn.

However, at a time when early childhood is so much under the spotlight, we have to ask ourselves whether there are certain essential aspects of life on which the well-being of such young children depends. We are all witnesses to young children's ability to use computers and other information technology. Most parents notice that by about eight months of age their babies cannot wait to take possession of the television remote control gizmo, as well as those traditional objects of desire – bunches of keys and purses. From a very early age children can recognise what gives a person power in their family or community and they want to have a share in that power.

In this book two research teams have joined forces to present cross-cultural evidence about another 'agent' of power with which most young children in societies where this is a potent force want to engage – that powerful 'agent' is print literacy.

Being literate enables and strengthens the ability to communicate, to gain access to and to understand other fields of knowledge, to be creative – to take existing knowledge and transform it. However, young children find many other ways to understand the world and to communicate. They explore, experiment, discover, represent, interpret, and create, through making sounds, using gestures, music, movement, building, model-making, painting, fantasy and role play. In the famous nurseries of Reggio Emilia in Northern Italy they argue that there are 'a hundred languages of children' (Edwards *et al.,* 1998). So why is it especially important to consider early literacy if young children (aged between birth and six years) have not been expected to be able to read and write until after the beginning of formal schooling? Might early literacy be a bad thing? Shouldn't we, as early childhood educators, be protecting children from too much pressure, too much formality too soon? The world may be changing fast but should we not ensure that children 'have a childhood'? Many educational researchers question the assumptions underlying the kinds of 'reforms' which have occurred in the policies of several countries (see for example, Docking, 2000).

In the next chapter we discuss the ways in which our assumptions about childhood, how we think about childhood – and what childhood is 'for' – impact on the kinds of provision we make for children's learning and the teaching approaches we adopt.

A few years ago one of us (Tricia) was visiting preschools in Denmark. It was apparent that very little attention was paid to early literacy. There were no captions or child-level notices, no materials for children's use for emergent literacy activities, no book corners. When asked whether Danish educators would offer anything of this nature, the response was one of seeing the UK as aberrant, as putting pressure on young children too early. This was frowned on by the Danish colleagues even when the activities offered were intended to be fun. The event caused a great deal of reflection and questioning about the nature of early childhood, literacy learning and life in print-dependent societies.

Now, in some countries, there is a spotlight on the youngest children and some politicians are pressing for children to be taught to read and to be numerate earlier in their lives. They believe that such an early start will give their children (and hence in time their economies) an advantage over those countries where literacy and numeracy have been left until later. Later learning is in turn linked with lower levels of achievement in the minds of politicians in some countries. While it is obvious that being literate and numerate are keys to other areas of understanding, it is not obvious that the earlier one is taught the mechanics of literacy and numeracy the more one will be successful in later life.

In her preparatory document for a television programme ('Despatches: Too Much Too Soon?' Channel 4, 1998), Claire Mills (1998) used evidence about the type of structured, play-based curriculum used in countries such as Belgium and Switzerland, where older pupils achieve highly successful literacy scores. There, formal literacy is left until the primary school, with admission at six. She argued further that in the UK there is no similar early years curriculum to build up the skills needed as a foundation for literacy and that 'top-down' formal literacy teaching will be counter-productive in the long run. In fact research already shows (Brooks *et al.,* 1997) that the countries where children are taught to read early, using formal teacher-led, instructional approaches, are those where later achievement is lower than in countries which, through play, lay structured foundations in their nurseries.

At the same time as there is a strong focus on early learning, many countries are increasing their provision of preschool and 'out-of-school-hours' care facilities, to enable parents to work. The realisation that young children's learning should be enhanced by attendance at pre-school settings, as well as the opportunities this affords governments to promote particular aspects of early learning (including literacy), are reflected in the amount of government attention (for example, in the USA the Clinton's White House seminar about early brain development; in England the production of a curriculum framework which must be adhered to in order to access government funding – SCAA, 1996; QCA, 1999). Thus, in Chapter 2 we discuss brain research and in Chapter 3 research evidence about early literacy.

Lifelong learning: early childhood education and care

Growing recognition that children's earliest years are an important phase in which the foundations of learning are laid has meant that the idea of lifelong learning, earlier taken to mean adults' continuing learning, really encompasses the whole of life, from cradle to grave. In, 1997, Ministers of Education of the member countries in the OECD (Organisation for Economic Cooperation and Development) decided that a twelve-country survey of Early Childhood Education and Care (ECEC) provision should be mounted. International teams would visit each country in turn and produce reports, which would eventually be combined into a book discussing the full twelve-country survey (to be published by the OECD in 2002).

What is especially significant about this study is, firstly, that it is being mounted by an organisation concerned with economic issues (that is, interested in childcare in order to accommodate parental employment, as well as the levels of education of future workforces). Secondly, this interest demonstrates the high profile of the very earliest years worldwide (with politicians asking if the potential of the earliest years is being 'wasted').

It is important to note that the OECD's intention is not to promote uniformity but to see each country's provision within its own historical and cultural context. However, policy-makers, practitioners and parents will no doubt wish to use the comparative data as fruitfully as possible and information about services in different countries can often be the catalyst to improvements in a country which has not committed as much thought and investment to its own services.

One of the problems likely to emerge from these reports is the variability of provision in the different countries (see also David, 1993, 1998; Oberhuemer and Ulich, 1997). In particular, as Angela Anning and Anne Edwards (1999) point out in relation to the UK, many early childhood educators feel vulnerable in the face of pressure to teach young children about what has been seen traditionally as the domain of the primary school curriculum. This vulnerability is hardly surprising when one realises the lack of investment in the education and training of ECEC professionals in many countries to date.

Theorising about young children learning

The child development theories which have been relied upon to inform practice in the early years field were not necessarily intended to be used in this way – we discuss influential child development and learning theories in Chapters 2 and 3. However, the influence of theory can be seen in the beliefs and practices of teachers in nursery settings and the sharp contrast with the more formal teaching styles of primary school is evidence of different models of learners in the two fields in several of the countries we studied. Teaching styles in traditional nursery education have been labelled 'child-centred' and this is variously interpreted. Of course, some primary schools have adopted child-centred approaches but the evidence from UK reports shows that even when this type of approach was strongly advocated by government documents, only around one primary school in ten adopted it (HMI, 1978).

In a child-centred approach, the child takes the lead and initiates activities, with the adult taking a supporting role, fostering the child's efforts to learn by providing appropriate materials and being on hand to assist, prompt, question, or explain as necessary. This type of approach is always attributed to the application of the theories of Jean Piaget (see, for example, Piaget, 1955), where the child is portrayed as a 'lone scientist' interacting with and finding out about the world, and through play assimilating new material into existing cognitive structures. Further play practising the new activity is then thought to promote learning, as the child's cognitive structures accommodate it. In this model of learning children actively initiate and struggle to achieve the understandings they set themselves. This theory has implications for practitioners, who must therefore provide an appropriate context for learning through being active (this can mean thinking as well as moving around and manipulating materials!). These contexts for learning will be set up to promote play and exploration (see further discussion in Chapters 3 and 6). In such environments, the adult's style contrasts with the model where the adult takes the lead and prescribes all the child's activities. According to the latter model, the adult is all-knowing and 'owns knowledge' which must be transferred to the child. It is what the poet Yeats described as a 'filling buckets' model of education.

Whether by accident or by design, we are passing on our cultural heritage to young children. They watch us carefully and from birth they are learning about how one operates in the home and community in which they find themselves. If we help them in this task, we are assisting in their co-construction of knowledge, their understandings of their world. They come to us with amazing capabilities, pre-programmed to be social, to communicate and to think/ reflect. By deliberately feeding that curiosity, promoting that desire to know and to learn, we are 'lighting fires' – Yeats' description of what education should be. Thus it is not only the play environment which requires careful planning: the adults who teach young children need to be given time to observe children, to discuss those observations in the light of research and theory, to reflect on what they have seen in their observations and what this tells them about the learning of the children concerned, and so come to understand how and when to intervene, rather than simply adopting a 'stand back and light the blue touch-paper approach' (David, 1990).

Theory and practice

We should not feel intimidated by published theory, nor feel that it is irrelevant to practice. For in everyday life with young children, parents and teachers are theorising too; it is just that they rarely write down their theories and present them to the world. For example, they may have a theory about early daycare being bad for babies, but this theory might be challenged by research carried out in daycare environments where the adults are suitably, and warmly, responsive to each baby's individual needs and carefully link their behaviours with those the baby experiences at home.

Sometimes our own theories are an amalgam of theories and research findings we have read about, sometimes we incorporate ideas derived from reflecting on close observation of children and educators in ECEC (Early Childhood Education and Care) over a long career, sometimes they are derived from our own early experiences. At the same time, our theories are affected by our values. If we believe children are people who should be respected from the moment of birth (and before), that belief influences our approaches to their learning. Similarly, if we believe literacy to be both a cognitive activity and to be socially constructed (Barton, 1994), to have different meanings in different societies or cultures, our own theory about how children become literate will be very different from that of a person who believes one needs to 'put into' children certain knowledge about print.

It is because we all theorise willy-nilly that we need to be more conscious of the origins of our theories. We can then base our theories on reflections of real-life observations of children and of our own and colleagues' practice, reflections on research and theoretical literature, and reflections on the assumptions made in our particular culture about young learners and about literacy itself.

Play

In the chapters that follow, we present evidence about young children engaging in literate play. This evidence comes from the work of our two research teams and we are eternally grateful to all the practitioners, children and parents who enabled us to gain these insights in the four different countries and ECEC systems. We have found all our participants committed to helping young children learn in ways they find enjoyable. In all of the countries we found support for the notion that enjoyment and meaning are important ingredients of early learning. We also found strong support for learning through play. Play as the most appropriate approach to learning (and teaching) in the earliest years of childhood is supported by both research and by government documents (see, for example, DfEE, 1999a).

Play, or playful approaches to learning, have a number of advantages. These include:

- children have intrinsic motivation and curiosity to engage;

- the self-posed 'questions' of play activity are meaningful and relevant to the child (or children) involved;

- there are usually many possibilities in play, rather than a 'right answer' to be sought, so play is non-threatening, although it is often challenging;

- 'ownership' and control of the situation by the learners strengthens both motivation and learning;

- the 'what if? quality of play encourages creativity; rules can be invented and broken;

- much play is social, encouraging language development and inter-personal skills, although it can be solitary;

- different forms of play exercise the body and the mind – especially allowing for both sides of the brain to be developed. As Tina Bruce says, play is 'an integrating mechanism, which brings together all we learn, know, feel and understand.' (Bruce, 1991: 60);

- adults can join in and 'model' language and behaviour in play, while still allowing the children to take the lead (for example, by making an 'appointment' at the 'hairdressing salon' or 'garage');

- play is pleasurable!

Engaging in play and language interactions may not be the only way children can become adept at using symbols, but it is probably the most meaningful for children. In their play, young children actually demon-strate their ability to manipulate symbols. They will build a boat or a stage with large blocks, treat a visiting adult to tea (which may be made of sand or even be invisible), speak into a toy telephone, cradle a doll as a baby. Drawing on their experiences, their ability to create new situa-tions and new ideas is endless. This ability to symbolise in their play provides a foundation for decoding and using print, a system of symbols.

Teaching young children

When children are provided with opportunities to learn through play, the pedagogy becomes 'invisible'. We need to see children's play activities as a never ceasing flow, their way of making sense of relationships and the world, for themselves, as Harriet Strandell (2000) argues. However, she also warns that play can be used as a way of 'policing' children's activities, when certain kinds of play are given greater status or approval by the adults. In adopting an invisible pedagogy educators try to de-centre, to stand in the children's shoes and so promote learning through the children's self-chosen activities and interests, rather than through those imposed as a result of adult predilections. Thus educators must create an environment in which they can be professional and 'formal' in their heads or on paper in planning, assessing and recording, but playful and 'informal' in relation to the children's experiences.

Following their research project studying teachers using play approaches, Bennett *et al.* suggest:-

> The teacher's role is multi-faceted and includes stimulating language and conversational skills; helping children to create, recognise and solve problems; supporting cognitive challenge; modelling behaviour, skills and learning processes; and direct teaching of skills and knowledge, where appropriate. Thus children can acquire knowledge, make sense and construct meaning from their play so that it becomes educationa ... Wood (1988) suggests that teaching children to become more aware of the processes involved in learning increases their abilities to use and transfer their knowledge and skills between different contexts. These metacognitive strategies include memorisation, recall, reflection-on-action, evaluation, organising information, communication, and forward planning ... Children need to recognise the relationships between playing and learning in order to become successful players and learners. (Bennett et al., 1997: 129)

Similarly, Angela Anning and Anne Edwards (1999: 166) reported on their collaborative research with a group of practitioners:-

> Again and again we returned to the notion of the significance of the quality of interactions between adults and children and adults and adults in the workplace as the heart and soul of good professional practice ... A phrase ... 'joint involvement episodes', became a kind of mantra for the team when we focused on the 'pedagogy' of working with young children. We also recognised the importance of the degree of intimacy and emotional engagement between adults and children if they were to be meaningful to both parties. We recognised the importance of structuring high quality learning opportunities...But we became more and more convinced of the importance of adults following children's learning by careful observation as the precursor to leading children, through guided participation, towards new learning. (Anning and Edwards, 1999:166)

For a number of years early childhood educators have talked and written about *learning* more than they have about *teaching* and they have been seen as remiss for this. The reasons for their reluctance have been firstly, positive, in that they preferred to focus on children's learning and how they achieve. But there has also been a negative reason – the inter-pretation of 'teaching' as meaning a formal approach where the children sit in serried rows and are all engaged with the same teacher-initiated task or focus at the same time.

In addition to this, those early educators who are not qualified teachers in the formal sense shy away from appearing to claim the title for their activities, despite the fact that they are also fostering children's learning.

However, we detect a sea change in attitudes. As Cathy Nutbrown (1998: 16) states, 'The words used to describe work with and for young children indicate and influence practice and philosophy in early education.'

The word 'teaching' is used liberally, for instance in the guidelines con-cerning the new English Early Learning Goals, the framework for the curriculum for children aged from three to six (QCA, 2000). This is important, because the rest of the document emphasises play-based learning and the role of the adult. The right to define what is meant by 'teaching' in this phase of education is therefore being reclaimed. In this book we use the words teacher, preschool educator, and practitioner interchangeably and we have used 'she' to refer to an educator, despite the fact that we believe there should be more men in the sector – our form of expression merely reflects the current situation in all the four countries where we carried out our research.

Sara Meadows (1993) has argued that to become more effective, in other words to empower children through their learning, early childhood educators need to adopt a model of learning which is underpinned by Vygotsky's ideas. This is called a social-constructivist model of learn-ing. According to this model, children actively construct their know-ledge with the help of more knowing others. This means we are adding to the Piagetian model of the child learning like a 'lone scientist' a second aspect where the child's thinking and learning is embedded in social interaction and communication with others. Learners are inter-dependent. The social-constructivist model requires teachers to do more than provide an appropriate environment for play; they must proactively create and recognise 'teachable moments', and must mediate learning 'in the culture' by providing the language and the time for children to review what they have been learning, in order to make this more con-scious.

Further, teachers of young children need to be familiar with their pupils' home cultures, so that they can de-centre – 'put themselves in the children's shoes' – to make the play and learning opportunities truly relevant. This means educators have a special responsibility to engage with parents, to enter into real partnerships in which the adults as well as the children are seen, and see themselves, as learners. In Chapter 4 we explore the ways in which changing assumptions about young children's additional language learning and relevant play experiences can extend the educational opportunities of all children.

Making sense of early literacy

This book is an outcome of three linked international research projects, the Preschool Literacy Project in Victoria, Australia and the Literacy and Numeracy at Transition Project in Australia and Singapore, which were carried out by the team at Melbourne University, and the Early Literacy Links project in England and France, undertaken by the team at Canterbury Christ Church University College.

Both teams adopted an ecological model of child development (Bronfenbrenner, 1979; Anning and Edwards, 1999), in which the respective histories, cultural traditions, and economic and educational situations of each nation were taken into account. The project is therefore cross-cultural rather than comparative – although some comparisons can be made about certain facets of the studies. Like the research *Preschool in Three Cultures* by Tobin *et al.* (1989), our interest has been in trying to 'make sense' of the understandings held by early childhood educators in the four very different preschool systems. We used questionnaires, observations, interviews, group discussions and document analysis as data sources.

We observed the children in their early education and care settings and talked with teachers about their practices and intentions, and their own training and ideas about early literacy.

At certain times, we recognised that many activities, which appeared on the surface to have no connection with early reading/or writing, contribute to essential foundations for print literacy within a holistic curriculum. Like Kress (1997), we also recognised the 'multi-modal' nature of learning about print. Most of all we were aware of differences in approach dependent upon a number of factors, such as knowing the research evidence about early learning in general and about early literacy learning in particular.

We were also aware that the differences in the training of the educators, the ages of admission to primary school and the relationships between early years curricula and primary school curricula, together with parental pressure and expectations, shape what happens to young children in their respective settings.

At this point we will simply say that France is the only one of our four countries to employ graduate teachers in all nursery classes (qualified to work with children aged two to eleven years following five years of academic and practical study on university courses). In the other three countries the majority of early educators have qualifications from relatively short (two years at a college of further, rather than higher, education), or part-time, or in-service training. Children attending English nursery schools, classes and reception classes of primary schools in the public (maintained) sector are usually taught by a graduate teacher with specialist teacher training and equivalent qualifications to any other teacher in the system. In most cases where the training given has been limited, few educators have attended courses about young children's literacy learning.

In Australia, training emphasises a developmental model that focuses on children's interests and child-centred pedagogy, rather than on any more specific aspects of curriculum. In Singapore, training is achieved through a one-year Certificate and a two-year Diploma. Degree programmes are now available from overseas universities, but are not required at any level. More recently, the Ministry of Community Development in Singapore has required all preschool staff to upgrade to Diploma level by 2004.

The age at which children begin their primary school careers can have a profound influence on the opportunities they have for learning through play and, similarly, on the attitudes of early educators to incorporating literacy learning in their curricula. In Singapore and France children begin primary school at age six, in Australia at five, also the official age of admission in England. However, over the last few years, English primary schools have been admitting children into their reception classes (Year R) at the start of the academic year in which they become five. So there are children aged four years and one day in the reception classes of some English primary schools – in other words they are not in nursery classes. Clearly there would be no problem about the admission of such young children if the classes were called Year R but emulated the practice of nurseries, with appropriate staffing, curricula and space. We further discuss the pressures brought about by early admission to primary school and 'top down' or 'push down' expectations in Chapters 5 and 8.

In all the chapters that follow we have provided research information, together with examples – stories – of children engaging in literate play with the appropriate support of caring, committed teachers who accept that these exciting learners want to be part of their community. If it is a print-dependent community, helping them understand 'how print works', through their play, enables them to be powerful participants in the life of that community.

2
Changing childhoods

At their instigation, Coralie (4) and Eliot (just 2) are playing 'What time is it, Mr Wolf?' with their grandfather. Coralie and her Mum had found a story book about children playing this game in the local bookshop and Coralie was quickly able to use two voices in her telling of the tale – one for the children, another, gruffer one for the wolf. Grandad had taken up his role with care and as the two began to enquire, 'What time is it, Mr Wolf?' it became apparent that Eliot had transposed the 'Mr' to 'Little'.

C: What time is it, Mr Wolf?

E: (at same time and screwing up his face with the effort): Time is it Little Wolf?

G: (softly): One o'clock.

C: What time is it Mr Wolf?

E: (at same time, screwing up his face even more, more loudly): Time is it Little Wolf?

G: (softly): Two o'clock.

C: What time is it Mr Wolf?

E: (at same time, even louder and with more effort, more screwing up of the face): Time is it Little Wolf?

G: (a little more loudly): Three o'clock.

So the game goes on until it is 'dinner time' and Grandad chases the two squealing children into the porch, where they beg him for another game of Mr/Little Wolf and direct the manner in which it must be played.

So much can be learnt from play incidents like this. We realise that Eliot, at just two, has never heard anyone called 'Mr', so he transposes the word to one with which he is familiar. Both children know the sequence of the numbers from one to five and can predict 'dinner time', both can connect their game with the pictures (and for Coralie some of the print) in their book. How exciting it can be to bring to life what is found in the pages of a book – and vice versa. How fortunate these children are to have a grandfather living close by who understands the importance of play and talk and the role of 'more knowledgeable others' in young children's exhilarating struggles to make sense of their worlds – yet this is what we would probably wish for all young children. At home these children are being supported in their co-construction of their understandings of the world and of literacy, and their creative explorations of the characters and events. At the nursery they both attend they are similarly supported – but for some nursery age children and for many in primary school classes, pressure to achieve narrowly conceived targets means that inappropriate teacher-directed experiences are the norm, even at this early age. In this chapter we consider the consequences of a rigid, skills-based approach to literacy for children in the primary school and the ways in which constructions of childhood and of literacy influence teaching. Such considerations are vital for societies with a wish to promote the development of future artists, writers, scientists, inventors and entrepreneurs, since these and many other professions require creativity.

Children seem to have a disposition to be creative. They obviously learn much from the 'knowledgeable others' who provide knowledge through direct teaching about the areas of learning or disciplines (such as music). However, children 'transform' knowledge they have acquired through the 'instruction', or 'apprenticeship', as well as through their own exploration and play. If education systems 'kill off' creativity, perhaps they 'commit suicide' culturally and commercially.

Changing childhoods

Over the last century, philosophers and researchers have come to realise that children's physiological growth, although influenced by living conditions and diet, follows a fairly similar path no matter where the child lives, that human genetic patterns relating to biology are largely generalised. However, they also note that children in different societies, different circumstances, have been encouraged to develop different psychological features more strongly or weakly as a result of exposure to different societal demands. In other words, nature and nurture are interwoven and not separate forces for growth. Where in the past it had been argued that development was required in order for learning to be possible, learning is now thought to be an instigator of development and further development then stimulates further learning – so the two are also inextricably related (see for example Morss, 1990).

The way in which a particular society thinks about children and the expectations that society has of children at different ages are called 'constructions of childhood'. Even within our own lives we can see how childhood has changed and how this impacts on children and the curriculum they are offered in nurseries and schools. Childhood is a product of a particular time and place.

Adult conceptualisations of childhood have always influenced the activities we ask children to be involved with in our nurseries and schools. Some governments' visions for the uses of childhood have created skills- and knowledge-based emphases within schools, which can result in a reduction in the opportunity for children to be creative. Children's opportunities for self-conceptualisation through play and writing are under threat by this current adult-imposed use for our young's childhood experience. Children need to be given the chance to reflect upon themselves and their worlds through play, and later through their own writing.

> I am someone with the passionate belief that all of us, no matter how old or young, have the ability to reflect on who we are, what we do, where we come from, what others do to us, what might happen to us, what we hope for, what we see and hear and what we share. These may be our failures and successes, fears and losses, absurdities, shames, boasts, amazements, mysteries, yearnings and much more. Rosen and Barrs (1997:1)

The opportunity to reflect upon our own world is often an opportunity that is denied us. Our lives are dominated by the compulsion to work, think and utililise our talents and skills for others and we are forced to become, in body and soul, what those who hold our livelihood in their hands desire us to be. This is the world of work, the arena of citizenship, markets and economy. Here we argue that by ignoring our own place in the world we also put to one side our own conceptions of ourselves. This form of disorientation is encouraged early in our lives. The previous quotation is taken from an introductory chapter Michael Rosen wrote, encouraging children to write poetry (Rosen and Barrs, 1997). The belief expressed has its foundation in a particular conception of children, childhood, their abilities and their rights within society.

Conceptions of childhood have changed radically over time and place. Throughout history, they have been influenced mainly by religion, philosophy and economics. These understandings or 'constructions' of childhood have been reflected in our treatment of children in society and the assumptions on which the dominant constructions of childhood are founded are nowhere more obviously exposed than in a country's pre-schools and schools.

Here we set out to describe conceptions of children and their place within society at the start of the new millennium and intend to show how these 'constructions' of childhood are starkly exposed by the nature of the work we ask children to do within the classroom. Contemporary curricula seem obsessed with the future of adulthood rather than the 'now' of childhood.

Innocence and experience

There have been numerous perceptions of childhood over the last two centuries. All of these understandings have been influenced and changed by the dynamic economic and political nature of society (Hendricks, 1997). Historians seem to agree that 'ideas like parenthood and childhood are socially constructed and thus can be put together in diverse sets of ways' (Anderson quoted in Hendricks, 1997:35). These perceptions and conceptions of children have moved from extreme to extreme. For example, the child has been seen as the 'innocent' and the personification of a state of nature as asserted by the philosophers Locke and Rousseau. However, children were also subjected to the brutality and physical, psychological and sexual abuse of the industrialised age where the demand for profit overcame morality – or perhaps powerful groups in society did not perceive the children of the poor as similar to their own offspring. At the end of the eighteenth century very few voices were raised against the plight of the climbing boys and factory children whose lives were damaged by others' economic greed. (This is still the plight of a large proportion of children in the majority world of course.) 'For most children labouring was held to be a condition which would teach them numerous economic, social and moral principles' (Hendricks, 1997:39). Society is still trying to inculcate these same views through citizenship training, though hopefully by different teaching methods!

Fears of delinquency also influenced ideas of childhood. This fear brought a variety of Youthful Offenders Acts (1857, 1861 and 1866) in the UK. This perception of children – as young people likely to offend – arose out of anxieties about the effects of life in unsupervised gangs. Hendricks (1997) quotes one M.D. Hill, the recorder for Birmingham, in the 1850s:

> The latter [the delinquent] is a little stunted man already – he knows much and a great deal too much of what is called life – he can take care of his own immediate interests. He is self-reliant, he has so long directed or misdirected his own actions and has so little trust in those about him, that he submits to no control and asks for no protection. He has consequently much to unlearn – he has to be turned into a child again. (Hendricks, 1997:43)

Education was seen to be the means to bring such children to order. The need for education and the fear of delinquency were ideologically connected, even if not chronologically aligned. Schooling meant a radical shift in society's understanding of childhood. Knowledge was no longer that gained from life, and specifically from the factory or the street, but from school. Behaviour was normalised, often by pain of beatings, and it 'institutionalised the separation of children from society...the proper place for a child was in school' (Hendricks, 1997:46) – not in the factory. Society has always seen the importance of children and childhood and has always attempted to manipulate and control the childhood experience. James Britton in his work *Language and Learning* (1970) quotes a report written in 1925 by His Majesty's Inspectors. The report clearly sets out to persuade teachers of the need, through the medium of English, to imbue children with the language of school rather than the language of their own world:

> And when the subjects are such as deliberately throw them [children] into an atmosphere of their out-of-school life, it is almost certain that they will

express themselves in the language of the home and the street. English should be based upon what he reads and hears in school, and not until he has acquired some familiarity with the language, which the school is trying to build up, should he be asked to express himself upon other subjects. (HMI, quoted in Britton, 1970:19)

This view of English teaching discredits the child's use of language and invalidates the child's understanding of 'himself' and the culture that has surrounded 'him' before coming to school. English teaching was clearly seen as an important means of dispensing with self-conceptions through an attempted obliteration of home-received knowledge about language and the world. These 'other subjects' are the areas of interest that children want to write about – literacy domains which allow the act of writing to work with an empowering energy.

Contemporary views of childhood are also contested and changing, often in quite contradictory ways. On the one hand, constructions of childhood in the 1960s and 1970s began to view children as people with rights. Within schools, child-centred methods of teaching asserted the need to begin with the child and the knowledge s/he brought into the classroom. The work of Frank Smith (1978), Donald Graves (1983) and others reflected this in their suggestions about the way children should be asked to write. These authors were concerned with the need to encourage children to use writing as a means to express themselves, to be creative, rather than simply to re-present adults' ideas about the world.

In addition to this, in the years following the Second World War, international opinion expressed through the United Nations' Declaration of Children's Rights (UN, 1959) and later the Convention on the Rights of the Child (UN, 1989) led various organisations to champion children's rights within nation states (in the UK, for example, this included the Children's Legal Centre, Childline and the National Children's Bureau; in Australia, the Children's Commission in New South Wales). On the other hand, since the appalling murder of the abducted toddler Jamie Bulger by two older boys in Liverpool in 1993, public and legal attitudes to children among certain groups in England and elsewhere seem to be hardening again. However, it is important to remember that the two views of childhood may well have always coexisted, or the issue may not have generated the same reaction because most adults and children may have been equals.

Most governments now see their potential for national economic advancement in world markets as dependent upon a future workforce educated in very particular ways. In most advanced industrial and information societies, children's waking lives are regulated and organised for them and their freedom has been curtailed to an extent never known before (Hillman *et al*, 1990). Adult manipulation of the childhood experience has come to the fore with a severity not seen since children's direct involvement in industry in the eighteenth century.

It is true that various UK and Australian Government initiatives within education, intended to improve basic skills from an early age, indicate that childhood as an important phase in life in its own right, as a phenomenon and as an experience, is under threat. These initiatives in Australia include the Adelaide Declaration addressing the National Goals for Schooling (MCEETYA, 1999) and in England, the National Literacy Strategy (1998) and the National Numeracy Project (1999). But such initiatives appear to be rooted in a desire to prepare ever younger children for the adult world and the market place. It might be argued that childhood as conceptualised by contemporary policy makers is purely a 'bus stop' en route to adulthood. There is too little time for playfulness, individual expression, pleasure, laughter, mischief, self-reflection, to name but a few 'childish' traits. There is a danger that childhood culture and its self-realisation may be abandoned in favour of a passive reception of 'basic skills'. As a result, children may be given no time to express their own thoughts and ideas through experience of the 'now' in talk, in writing and, in some cases, even in the reading they are being asked to do in school.

Education, education and ...governments looking busy

Frank Coffield's *A Tale of Three Little Pigs: Building The Learning Society With Straw* (1997) provides today's teachers with some useful political and economic explanations for the changes they are experiencing within their classrooms. Coffield reflects upon government policy for combating unemployment and the need to rejuvenate the economy as a result of globalisation. The government within Britain points to the individual lack of skills within the workforce as the prime reasons for poor economic performance. Coffield quotes Edith Cresson speaking at the European Commission for Science, Training, Youth and Education.

She said: 'Every day thousands of people lose their jobs because their know-how is out of date' (Cresson, 1996, quoted in Coffield, 1997:21). As Coffield asserts, with the multiple reasons for unemployment such as:

> the relocation of industry to developing countries, automation and changes in production, international competition, lack of investment, high rates of interest, corporate downsizing etc. it is perverse to single out one particular reason (a lack of skills on the part of the individuals) to carry the burden of explanation. And if causation is considered to be a singular, then it will be no surprise if political remedies are narrowly conceived. (Coffield, 1997:2)

The UK and Australian governments seems to have responded to the perceived need for investment in human capital and have set education as the most important priority. Unable or unwilling to attempt to regulate other possible causes of economic poor performance, they concentrate on education. There are some who argue that the only area of policy left to the national governments of countries, either by bodies such as the European Community or by global capitalism, is in fact Education. 'But the continuing attraction of the theory of human capital lies in its comforting ideology which deflects attention away from the structural causes of poverty onto individuals' (Coffield, 1997:5). These individuals include the children who inhabit our classrooms on a daily basis – but at what cost to a child's right to creativity and the time to live the life of a child? The prevalent pressure leading to the dominant construction of childhood for the new millennium presents itself as a responsibility to prepare for the future and for the prosperity of the nation. Training in the basic skills of numeracy and literacy becomes the key to an affluent twenty-first century. The children of this new century must carry this heavy burden. For government, children's achievement makes or breaks them.

In some schools in Britain impossible targets are being set. For example, in one school of around 100 pupils aged between four and eleven, 97 per cent of the children being tested in their final year must reach or exceed a particular level in literacy which is set externally (known as level 4). This would mean that the school could only afford one child being assessed as reaching below level 4! Teachers are being forced to concede that time spent in school must be used to make reaching these targets the priority. Individual creativity, communication and self-expression are seen as expensive and distracting pastimes, despite long-standing evidence that schools in which children experience a broad and balanced curriculum, taught using stimulating approaches, actually do better on tests of academic achievement (for example, HMI, 1978).

Making sense of children's learning

In 1905 a report by women inspectors of schools for the UK included an observation by one of those inspectors, Kathleen Bathhurst, who recognised the need for young children to actively 'make sense' of what was being taught, rather than being expected to digest chunks of disembedded teacher-imposed content unrelated to their current interests and concerns. She wrote:

> Let us now follow the baby of three years through part of one day of school life. He is placed on a hard wooden seat (sometimes it is only the step of a gallery) …He often cannot reach the floor with his feet and in many cases he has no back to lean against. He is told to fold his arms and sit quiet…At a given signal every child in the class begins calling out mysterious sounds …I have actually heard one baby class repeat one sound a hundred and twenty times continuously … Bathurst 1905, in Van der Eyken, 1975:121)

As the twentieth century progressed, psychologists contributed to the debate about early learning. Jean Piaget corresponded with Susan Isaacs, while she was running her experimental nursery school in Cambridge and afterwards when she took up her inaugural post as a tutor in child development and education at the London University Institute of Education. Piaget's theory, like many other child development theories which have been relied upon to inform practice in the early years field, was not originally intended to be used in this way.

Children in early years settings in countries which adopted a Piagetian model of learning would be expected to explore their environment and everything in it, learning through first hand experience. However, during the latter part of the twentieth century, both psychologists and educationists began to recognise that the 'lone explorer/investigator' model was insufficient to explain children's learning. As Geekie *et al.* (1999) suggest:

> Children learn to see the world through the eyes provided by their culture…
> It is not just categories and labels which are learnt but also culturally specific

ways of communicating and thinking and solving problem ... The child is... learning to participate in the way his culture thinks about things...What children learn is essentially what their culture offers them, through the intervention of others...through collaborative sessions. Geekie et al. (1999: 9–10)

In other words, the 'more knowledgeable' others, who may be both adults and children, help children learn because as babies they come into the world 'pre-programmed' to want to participate in what is going on around them, to communicate and to be social. This is not to say that the influence of culture is simple, nor that children's development is completely determined by those around them in some kind of Frankenstein-ish way! It is important to remember intra-child characteristics as well as the ecology of the context in which they are growing and learning. Most babies and young children are quickly aware of the aspects of their society that have prestige and endow power and they will themselves seek to acquire the necessary knowledge, usually through engaging with the more knowledgeable others.

The main theorist to focus on these cultural and collaborative aspects of early learning was the Russian, Lev Vygotsky. Sadly, his work did not become widely known in the West until some 30 years after his death. He emphasised the social nature of learning, the ways in which children need the support of 'more knowing others' (who may be other children, as well as adults) and the importance attached to the adult's attention to what the child is trying to learn, what might be the next step in that learning, and how the adult can present the learning experience for the child to access (Vygotsky, 1978). In particular, Vygotsky argued that the social interactions, use of imagination and of one object to represent another (symbolic transformations) in play are highly complex processes which can lead to more advanced forms of cognition.

Vygotsky's theory sparked ideas in the West. Thus, research and writing by Bruner (1986), Nelson (1986) and Wood (1988) has further informed our knowledge base about the ways in which young children learn and how parents, other children and attentive educators 'scaffold' that learning.

Meanwhile, Howard Gardner's work on the theory of multiple intelligences accords with the Reggio Emilia approach, that there are myriad ways in which children 'make sense', express themselves and communicate with each other and with the adults around them (see for example Gardner, 1991). But it is the familiarity, the 'common knowledge' (Edwards and Mercer, 1987) in which these relationships are embedded, that enables the adults to interpret and understand children's meanings, and sometimes their delightful misconceptions.

> Only recently, as her speech has become clearer, it became obvious that Coralie, when singing Diddle diddle dumpling, my son John, had devised her own version of the nursery rhyme based on her experience at the time she learnt it. Since the age of two she had recited it perfectly adequately – or so it seemed – until her Mum realised she was in fact singing 'Diddle diddle dumpling mice and John'. The riotous image created, the idea of John going to bed with lots of cuddly little mice (for Coralie has watched them in their cages in the pet shop during the last two years) makes perfect sense. At the age of two she had little if any experience of anyone using the word 'son', nor can one be sure she had heard much about 'sons' or even 'daughters' by the age of four (especially in a way she would relate to the rhyme), and so the meaning she had made of it had stuck.

Similarly, children's dispositions, preferred 'intelligences', may influence the routes they take to fluency in language, both spoken and written, and it must be remembered that children may vary much more in how they learn to read and write than in their acquisition of spoken language, which seems to have a 'biological' basis (see, for example, Trevarthen, 1992).

So it is with this intimate knowledge of the home culture and the child's interests that a familiar adult and a child can together co-construct the child's understanding of their world – and of language and literacy.

> One morning early, preparing breakfast, Eliot (aged two) decided he wanted to help make a cup of tea for Grandad and he wanted one himself too. Grandad's mug was set in place, with a tea bag in it. A second mug was found for himself, but as he put it next to Grandad's, Nana said 'Oh, you might not want that one, it's got a chip in it' (That is, it was a pottery mug which had lost a small piece on the lip). Eliot's response was to stare quizzically into the bottom of the mug (looking for the French fry). Nana explained about that kind of chip and Eliot's total attention was then devoted to sorting through the crockery cupboard to try to find further chipped pots.

So familiar adults are important because they know about children's earlier experiences, they can help children build on what they know – they can 'scaffold' the child's next attempts and they can act as 'memory bank', recalling for the child not just what they learnt on a previous occasion and why they wanted to learn it but also how they learnt it – they can encourage metacognition.

We pointed out in chapter 1 that our research is based on the ecological theory of Bronfenbrenner (1979). His contribution to the field is important because it sought to combine ideas from sociology – about the impact of the environment and society in which children grow and develop – with ideas about children's inherent abilities and drives to learn (Bronfenbrenner and Morris, 1998). This theory recognises the interplay between children's dispositions to learn, the opportunities and experiences with which they are provided, and the wider context in which the adults closest to them are attempting to provide for their lives and learning.

Early brain development

Another area of current debate is that of brain development research and how it informs our understanding of young children and their learning.

Neurophysiologists are currently reticent about the findings of brain research, despite the fact that some in their ranks in the USA have declared the years from birth to three absolutely crucial for later learning. While most would argue that the period from birth to three is very important and that it is advantageous for children to have positive, stress-free experiences, neurophysiologists are keen to point out that brain development, the making of millions of neural connections as a result of experiences can still be achieved later – in other words, it is not a 'once for all' event, because the human brain is very 'plastic'. However, the brain is at its most plastic in those earliest years and playful encounters with loving adults are now recognised to be important more than they were in the days when babies were put out for long sessions sitting in prams, and largely ignored (Meade, forthcoming). However, over-stimulation (such as using flash cards with very small children) and constant bombardment are not what is called for. Babies will benefit from being treated as if they are people trying to make sense of the world and to be initiated into the culture. As we stated above, babies seem to be born 'pre-programmed' to want to communicate and to be social, and Trevarthen's research (1992) has demonstrated this.

Additionally, recent research by cognitive psychologists (whose discipline forms a 'bridge' between neurophysiology and education) is demonstrating the ways in which young children's brains need interactions with other brains in order to learn and develop (Gopnik *et al.*, 1999). Their work emphasises the importance of the 'zany uncle' (suggested by the psychologist Urie Bronfenbrenner) and other children, because these people will offer challenges to the child's understanding in ways that a straightforward carer may not. The cognitive scientists argue that these challenges cause the child's brain to be reprogrammed, perhaps even redesigned. They also suggest that play is the most appropriate vehicle for such challenges.

Assumptions about young learners, and their consequences

Each society holds particular assumptions about young children and what they need to be proficient in ways that society values. Our assumptions can hinder us from seeing that what we do may be harmful to some or to all the children who undergo an experience dictated by these assumptions. For example, in a 'spare the rod and spoil the child' culture it is possible that some children will become monsters, as Alice Miller (1987) showed in her study of Hitler's early life.

Similarly, if we believe because of custom that small children should not be expected to engage with literacy, we may be depriving them of access to understandings, which will underpin their later, more formal learning in primary school. What matters is the teaching approach adopted, its appropriateness for the phase of life and its relevance to the individual child. To assume that a small child can make sense of decontextualised teacher-talk about print (if only the teacher tells it 'correctly') is to misunderstand the child's co-construction of knowledge about literacy. However, if we assume (and base our assumptions on research evidence) that babies and young children really are trying to 'make sense' of their world, then play offers the most relevant mode of learning.

Writing in the here and now – children conceptualising themselves

So we come to the point where we ask ourselves why we want children to be print literate. If children have been identified as the most important asset to improved economic wealth and if childhood is seen as a 'place' where time must be spent training them in basic skills, schools become merely 'houses of instruction'. This view of education, concerned only with a potentially misconceived notion of how to improve their wealth, could be construed as a sign that we are, once again, beginning to ignore childhood as being an important period of emotional and creative growth. The nature of the work we are asking children to do in class-rooms and nurseries is apt to reflect this view. How and what we ask children in primary schools to write directly displays our own conceptions of children and childhood.

The belief that children can write anything worthwhile is still a relatively new one. In addition to the pressures to give play and creative writing-time second place to basic skills training, there are also those who feel strongly that children lack the emotional maturity to express and write pieces of value and significance. This is especially marked in discussions about children's ability to write poetry. An example of this thinking is demonstrated by Vernon Scannell's provocative assertion quoted by Sedgewick (1997): 'Young children do not write poems, and never have done… A poem is the exploration and shaping of experience… And to make a poem, a real poem, demands intelligence, imagination, passion, understanding, experience…and knowledge.' (Scannel, 1977 quoted in Sedgewick, 1997: 74-75) One wonders if Scannel has any experience of being and living with young children whom he claims have none of these attributes!

However his sentiments have been echoed in a number of comparatively recent views of writers and educationalists (Reeves, 1965; Hall, 1989). Fortunately, there is an increasing group expressing the strong convic-tion that children, given the opportunity to examine their own condition and the world around them, are well able to express their ideas and imaginings in powerful ways, including their own writing (Grainger and Lambirth, 1999). This power emanates from asking children to *con-ceptualise themselves as children* rather than to let others do it for them.

Children need to be asked to draw upon their own culture, interests and concerns, rather than being expected to write like the adults they may become, or the adults the grown-up world would like them to become. In other words, children's creativity is embedded in the *now*, not the *then*. Teachers of older children may need to dispense with the 'normal' tired subjects of school-imposed verse like 'Autumn', 'Fireworks' and 'Snowflakes' and replace it with the world of the young, as perceived and conceived by children themselves. So what will children write about? Here is an example.

> I Love
> I love playing Tekken 2 on my Playstation
> People getting hit by lightning fast attacks.
> Shouts of pain and distinctive battle losses
> My heart beating 100 million times a second and
> Then suddenly dropping to 2 times a second.
> People talking in a non-intelligible language.
> While saying to myself in hope,
> "Come on, come on".
> I'm thinking about if I win whom I will be fighting next.
> I'm daydreaming about winning and what they would say after the battle.
> Sam (Year 5 – age 9+)

'I Love' helps us to understand the passion and excitement felt by children sitting behind a computer game console. This is a poem that is unafraid to declare the 'pleasure factor' involved in new technological games. This poem places the reader nearer an 'authentic voice' of the child. The fear that many of us hold is that time is increasingly being eroded during which children can be given the opportunity to 'conceptualise' their own childhood through their writing.

Michael Rosen (1989) has described how writing empowers the writer in a number of ways;

- It helps the writer preserve events and happenings, but puts the writer 'centre stage' (Rosen, 1989). Writing allows us to manipulate those events as we want, to change things when necessary and play around with them, sometimes – awesome events.

- The writer is able to reflect on the world. A comparison can be made between the written experience and how it was remembered before it was written down (Rosen, 1989). Writing helps us describe our own perceptions and our own conceptions of this world run by adults.

• Writing opens up avenues to start conversation. When children write, the adults around them have the chance to discuss children's feelings and perceptions of events and happenings: 'By treating it as real and valid now, we acknowledge that the child is not simply a pre-adult with incomplete or immature feelings. We give the child the possibility of valuing his or her own experience' (Rosen, 1989: 35).

The result of allowing children to reflect upon their own condition, their own place within society and upon those who have care over them, makes their writing both powerful and sometimes disturbing and challenging to the conceptions of childhood adults may hold. Real children's voices do not necessarily reflect the views of adults who see children as innocents or as 'learning machines' preparing for the adult world of the market. Indeed, when children reflect upon anger and shame, love and divorce, food and families (the world seen and conceptualised and perceived by themselves), they often 'hold the mirror up' to adult behaviour and reflect proverbial weakness and observed failings. Their own voices can be raw and rowdy, hoarse and hard, and may challenge adults both in content and in their contemporary phrases, swear words and regional dialects (Grainger and Lambirth, 1999).

The fears expressed by the Recorder of Birmingham in the 1850s come to mind when anticipating the responses of some adults when reading this kind of writing. The child may well be perceived as not behaving as children should within the classroom; they may be failing to live up to expectations. Perhaps Stephen, whose poem is reproduced below has much to 'unlearn' and needs to 'learn to be a child again'.

'Mum'
'What?'
'I'm bored'
'Why don't you play on your computer?'
'No'
'Why?'
'That's boring'

'Go out and play football'
'No'
'Why?'
"Cos we've just been playing football, and it's boring'
'Well, go and clean the toilet, then tidy your room, then...'
'I'll play on my computer'
'I thought it was boring'
'It bloody ain't now!'
'Get to your room!'
'Arrrr Mummmm:'
'Now!'
'IT AIN'T FAIR!'

Children are experts on topics like boredom and family feuds. Allowing children to write on these subjects empowers them to write about the world from their own stance and from their own perceptions. There would be a number of red marks and crossings out on this piece of writing from a teacher determined only to prepare Stephen for the world of work.

Literacy and play

The government should be praised for its determination to raise standards of achievement and for many of the commendable elements within the focus on literacy; it is not the intention of this chapter to add directly to other criticisms. However, if those involved with children's learning wish to protect the interests of children in classrooms, then they must consider the need to allow children's culture to flourish within school and give time for children to consider themselves through their writing.

The UK's National Literacy Strategy has already been comprehensively criticised for both its weak research base and its content (Hilton, 1998; Dombey, 1998; Carter, 2000). For instance, Dennis Carter has made some chilling observations with respect to the effects of a curriculum aimed only at improving basic skills: 'Many children are bored, their teachers burdened with too much tedious planning, their parents anxious about their children's waning levels of interest' (Carter, 2000:2). Carter views the NLS as a threat to the opportunity for children to play: 'The kinds of play relevant when we consider literacy are those concerned with the imagination, play with language, visual play, the development of a creativity in handling words, ideas and feelings' (Carter, 2000:3) Amongst other things this means the chance to play with understandings about their world, their direct environment and their place within it. It means the opportunity to make public their perceptions and conceptions of themselves now.

The new millennium offers many challenges to all those within society. Clearly developed societies are in the middle of far-reaching technological changes (Kress, 2000). With these changes come the inevitable anxiety and concern from governments, but also anxieties from the citizens who inhabit this changing environment. As usual, 'language use and all other aspects of linguistic practice come to serve as powerful metaphors for the reimposition of stability and control' (Kress, 2000:12).

In the clamour to gain control, governments and the teachers who have been given the huge responsibility to work for the future prosperity of nations need to remember the individual children's desire to be themselves in the here and now. They need to give children the opportunity to express this conceptualisation of themselves. In the early years this can be achieved through their play and creative activities – what in the famous Reggio Emilia nurseries are called 'the hundred languages of children' (Edwards *et al.*, 1998) – and in the later years through writing for and about themselves.

3

What do we know about young children and literacy?

Introduction to thinking about early literacy

Teachers know well what theory and research is now illuminating. No two children learn literacy in exactly the same way, what works for one child does not necessarily work for another, similar programmes advantage different children in different ways, and some children unexpectedly succeed while others unexpectedly have difficulty during their early years of schooling. Is this to do with the complexities specific to literacy learning, or is it because of the nature of learning itself, particularly during the early years of childhood?

Multiple perspectives on what constitutes learning and learning literacy are helpful in unravelling some of this complexity. We understand that there will be numerous cognitive processes involved; visual and auditory processing strategies, short-term memory, attention and the like. There will be emotional factors to do with disposition, motivation and confidence in having a go. There will be physical factors associated with sight, hearing, tiredness, hunger and well-being. There will be issues around available resources, responsive adults and timing. There will be other issues associated with previous experiences and their relevance and appropriateness, as well as the macro-systems of nation and community. What kinds of learning in general, and literacy learning in particular, are valued by significant others, used and shared within the child's life experiences? Who models, demonstrates and facilitates different activities, including literacy, during everyday life?

To reduce learning to read and write in particular, and literacy learning in general, to a set of classroom readers, the alphabet or other procedures is clearly inappropriate. Children learn about literacy and how to read and write in many different ways. Teachers know and understand that no one method or approach will suit all learners. As Marie Clay (1998) reminds us, children move *By Different Paths to Common Outcomes*. These 'different paths' will be dictated by all the multitude of experiences and features, some listed above. No two children experience the world in exactly the same way, and no two children have exactly the same temperament or physical attributes. These aspects of individuality interrelate throughout a multitude of socially and culturally valued ways that add up to the developmental diversity, which characterises many differences within a common framework of humanity.

Major contributions to our understandings

During the 1960s new concepts of learning emerged (Hunt, 1961). The importance of early stimulation for learning was emphasised and pointed up the significance of Bruner's statement that 'any subject can be taught effectively in some intellectually honest form to any child at any stage of development' (Bruner, 1960). These views, in conjunction with those of Vygotsky, which were just becoming known through translation, heralded the way forward to what we now understand as the social construction of knowledge.

As we explained in Chapter 1, Vygotsky's work influenced others and provided the impetus for social constructivist understandings, through his statement: 'what a child can do with assistance today she will be able to do by herself tomorrow' (1978:87).

These views extended the notion of children as lone scientists hypothesising about the world and further exploring on their own, the position based on the interpretation of Piaget's ideas (1955), by arguing firstly, that children were learning all the time and could be taught at any age; and secondly, that they learned skills particularly by engaging in appropriate activities with more knowledgeable, significant others. This position was especially important for people working with children who experienced any difficulties in learning. Groups of specialist professionals emerged at this time, dedicated to early intervention with the least able children.

These developments in thinking had a profound impact during the, 1970s. Researchers (for example, Goodman, 1967; Clay, 1969,, 1975) and others began to take notice of the activities of young children. They observed children learning and they observed them learning literacy. They reported the sophistication of very young children: how these learners drew on all kinds of information about print in their environment and meshed these experiences with what they already knew about language and ways of making sense of their world.

During the 1980s a great deal of interest was shown in how very young children constructed literacy from their experience of literacy around them and others using literacy for their own purposes. Studies during this time (for example, Bissex, 1980; Taylor, 1983) contributed further to this view of literacy as social construction. Ferreiro and Teborosky gave their interpretation:

> The children we know are learners who actively try to understand the world around them, to answer questions the world poses...It is absurd to imagine that ...children growing up in an urban environment that displays print everywhere (on toys, on billboards and road signs, on their clothes, on TV) do not develop any ideas about this cultural object until they find themselves sitting in front of a teacher [at school]. (1983:12)

During the 1980s and 1990s the study of literacy has taken on a much broader perspective (Barton, 1994). Early literacy and its further development in young children is considered more inclusive of children's experiences of the world and their ability to make meaning from their environment (Hall, 1987). As Cairney has emphasised, 'the meanings we build as we read and write are our experiences, our knowledge about the world, and also our reasons for developing them in the beginning' (1995:2).

Types of discourse and the way we read and write them are the social constructs of specific groups. Individuals are enculturated into these practices and these meanings. The development of literacy is, therefore, a profoundly social process. McLane and McNamee (1990) show how it is embedded in social relationships, especially in children's relationships with people in their immediate family, grandparents, friends, care givers and teachers. These are the more knowledgeable, significant others who act as models, provide the materials, demonstrate, offer support, establish expectations, instruct, encourage and reward effort. Through this perspective, literacy is seen to develop through children's relationships with their immediate care givers; it then broadens and is expressed and elaborated through their wider community – in the neighbourhood, the local community and other prior-to-school settings, and finally through the formal programmes encountered in schools.

Understanding and learning

What is now clearly established is the diversity of experience and difference which characterises young children's learning generally and literacy learning in particular. Olson (1994, 1998) indicates how modern cognitive psychology explains behaviours in terms of what children are doing, or trying to do, or think they are trying to do. This striving is pertinent to early literacy development. Indeed, *intentionality* has now taken the place of *causality.* Therefore, the effects of instruction are not seen as the simple outcomes of applying certain procedures to learners with certain characteristics. Learners have intentional states, including beliefs, goals and feelings. Once this is recognised, the whole pedagogical enterprise changes its focus from producing 'effects' to helping learners achieve *their* goals.

The critical concept here is 'understanding' and the role of the teacher is not simply to produce some effects in a learner, but to produce understandings. In this view 'errors' are seen as misunderstandings rather than as failures to learn. The question moves from 'What can't this child do?' to 'What is this child trying to do?', 'What is this child understanding or misunderstanding?' This suggests that it is easier for a learner to understand what their teachers say when there is an existing understanding of what they are talking about. In this sense, children who are categorised as low achievers in school are now deemed to have limitations in their understandings, and perhaps their experiences, rather than any defective learning abilities. This has been an important breakthrough for practice in early childhood education, as yet to be fully realised.

Questions are now being asked concerning how best to create and develop these understandings, and to gain an insight into where they come from, rather than condemning children or their families to various categories of ineducability because of learning difficulties. What is clear is that understandings do not come from systematic and specific instruction, because that in turn requires prior understandings. Understandings come from more general experience of the topic in which the learning takes place. We learn initially by engaging in activities where we are helped to understand what is going on, and supported by more knowledgeable others. This insight is profound but still needs to be universally accepted by early childhood educators.

Thus, we already know that children who come to school from actively literate backgrounds, where they are engaged with print in a wide variety of forms, are more likely to make rapid progress in learning to read and write through formal instruction when they arrive in school. What is it about these actively literate homes that gives them this head start? One of the things that is happening for these children is that they are included in a high number of socially and culturally relevant literacy events, from joining in sending and signing messages, for instance, to making lists, owning and sharing printed materials, listening and talking about stories and the like. It is through these experiences that children develop the conceptual understandings concerning literacy that will be appropriate precursors to more formal instruction.

Clay (1975:7) identifies that the more 'awareness' children have of print before entering school, the easier it will be for them to learn what is taught in the first year of school. She emphasises that awareness is a key concept for educators who work with children making the transition from spoken language to written language. Indeed, what children learn depends on their families and the communities they live in and, importantly, what they choose to pay attention to. In this respect each child's early experiences will be relative to the cultural norms of their social group and this will need to be considered when identifying the understandings of any particular child. Only performance is observable, but it must serve as a basis for inferring underlying learning processes and understandings.

When we observe and listen, and try to understand what it is that the child understands, we are trying to work with the child's perspective in mind, not our own. This is not the same as having a curriculum (pre-school or school) where there may be a sequenced plan of instruction bearing little relationship to the different understandings of different children who will be travelling different paths. As Katz and Chard (1988) have pointed out, a homogeneous curriculum leads to hetero-geneous outcomes and if systems want homogeneous outcomes they will need to provide for heterogeneous opportunities for learning.

- Children learn the same things in different ways.

- Children learn with the support of more knowledgeable others.

- Children learn through perspectives provided by their family, and by social and cultural contexts.

- Understanding precedes learning:

- Underlying processes are not always obvious or observable.

Literacy learning prior to school

If preschools do not provide opportunities for literacy experiences this will result in little literacy awareness on the part of those children who come from homes and communities with little or few experiences of literacy. If early childhood professionals in the variety of prior-to-school settings choose to ignore literacy, they will demonstrate models of people who choose to ignore literacy activities. However,

preschool educators do not agree on whether, and how, to foster literacy awareness; some are committed to having children learn their letters to give them a good preparation for entry into school, while others would leave children unaware of the existence of such things until faced with school instruction. (Clay, 1998:43)

Significant shifts have taken place in theory, research, policy and prac-tice, although not always in alignment one with the other. We have moved from the early conceptions of 'pre-reading' and 'pre-writing' which emphasised skill development outside of a print context, we have moved from 'readiness' that emphasised waiting for maturation, through notions of emergent literacy which focused on environmental and social print in context, towards early literacy which captures the essence of developing awareness and understanding of the wider functions and variety of both writing and reading. This later discourse highlights the child's active construction of increasingly more sophisticated and con-ventional literacy strategies used within the social and cultural context of their life.

Yaden *et al.* (1999) have reviewed this 'polyphony of perspectives' and cite research where systematic and explicit attempts to teach young children specific skills thought necessary for reading and writing have not been successful in either keeping their attention or leading to later achievement. However, naturalistic observations of children's spontaneous dramatic play (Neuman and Roskos, 1991) have indicated that children often incorporate literate behaviour as part of the play scripts they invent. Nevertheless, Morrow (1991) found in her study of 35 kindergarten classrooms (in the US with five to six year olds) many of these settings were not well designed to facilitate literacy behaviours. Few literacy materials were easily available for children to use and teachers did little to promote authentic literacy activities during play.

As a consequence of these studies and many others like them (for example, Walker, *et al.,* 1997; Neuman and Roskos, 1997; Kantor *et al.,* 1992), educational researchers began to investigate the development of literacy-enriched play centres. These enriched centres are marked by the addition of general literacy materials such as pencils and paper, books and other printed materials, as well as theme-related literacy props. A major premise underlying this work is that play interventions can have a direct impact on written language development by providing opportunities for children to read and write in contextualised situations (Hall, 1987). Play centres are complex ecological places where the context of the play activity is socially constructed by those involved. Adults are not necessarily excluded from these settings, rather they adopt multiple roles in the course of these events as opposed to operating within a single interaction style (Roskos and Neuman, 1993; Schrader, 1991).

Pickett (1998) reports her study of a literacy-enriched play setting, in this case the block corner. She reported a modest increase in literacy activities (4:1) when compared to the non-enriched setting and a major increase (51:1) when an adult model was introduced. Because children tend to incorporate their own experiences and knowledge into their play, it is not surprising that some of them with little experience and awareness of literacy in their lives may be unable to incorporate literacy spontaneously. Pickett's study confirms other studies (cf. Morrow, 1990; Morrow and Rand, 1991) where the children were seen to create and communicate using print after discussion and collaboration with an adult. These children were more willing to write when an adult was available to stimulate and assist their efforts.

Play as context and process

Play, in an appropriately enriched environment, is clearly a valuable part of the early childhood literacy curriculum. However, play alone will not necessarily address development and progression towards educationally valued behaviours. Teachers do need to be involved with the children during the course of their play for this to happen. Involvement here does not mean that teachers either direct or take over the play, rather there is a need to observe the children and create appropriate environments in order to extend knowledge and model literate strategies appropriately.

Continuing to use play as a medium, Rowe (1998) observed two- to three-year-olds responding to books. Book-related play served as a means of inquiry where these young children could safely create and test solutions to their own problems. Book-related dramatic play was found to be much more than a context for becoming aware of literacy, it served as an important part of literacy learning processes. As teachers and children took on roles in play, they provided important feedback confirming, and sometimes challenging, the children's perspectives about the world portrayed by books and their own world of experience. Dramatic play of this kind tended to serve as a connecting link, a bridge between the child's world and that of the adult, represented by books and the book-reading events in which they were embedded (Einarsdottir, 1996).

As a result of studies like these, young children are no longer seen as participants in a maturational process that gets them 'ready' to read; rather they are seen as active constructors of their own literacy knowledge and understandings through a long process of becoming literate that begins from birth.

In their description of a classroom context for reading and writing, Teale and Martinez (1989) emphasise that formal literacy activities themselves do not make for a literacy curriculum; rather it is the many ways in which teachers help children make those bridges between what is being done in the classroom and reading and writing in their everyday world. Clearly, these connections are best made as literacy is woven in and through the fabric of classroom life. Literacy takes on shape, pattern and texture as it is constructed to meet the interests and needs of individuals and groups of children. The broader implication here is that a literacy curriculum in early childhood settings needs to respect and reflect the nature of daily life as it is experienced and understood by different children within particular settings.

From research to practice

The years from birth to six, the early years at home and at school, are the most important for developing the foundations for later success in an education system which relies on written language through books and written work for progress and assessment. Learning, in the 'developed' societies of the world, is evaluated through high levels of both articulation and literacy. These processes are the business of powerful human interaction and the foundation of valued social and intellectual transactions. They are defined by cultural protocols and passed on from one generation to the next. All children, therefore, should have access to this cultural transmission. This is an issue of equity, social justice and the further development of humankind.

How then, are these skills and abilities passed on to our youngest children? Because we all speak at least one language fluently and most of us use writing effortlessly for personal and social purposes it is sometimes hard for us to focus on and understand the processes involved. It can be even more difficult to grasp the significance of the behaviours of young children as they learn to speak and to write and read. This is because language is opaque to us and we use it easily to convey and share meanings surrounding our daily lives. For instance, we do not spend time parsing sentences into parts of speech when we phone for a taxi or call out to our children to come indoors.

Explicit teaching of these elements of language alone, out of context, will not necessarily achieve success with uses of language. This is because the meanings, the communicative force of language, is independent of the words themselves. The words act as a code and are linked to meanings through complex rule systems. Indeed, behaviour, in whatever form, is highly patterned and it is always worth remembering that nothing we, or our children, do is random. What we need to learn to do better is the skilful and sensitive questioning and provision of activities which will help children to reveal how they are working things out for themselves, and we will learn to do this if we observe them carefully while we listen to them.

Features of language

Language is a distinctly human form of patterned behaviour; it is highly ordered and rule-governed. What children learn as they learn language is the sophisticated ways in which layers of language function and how these layers interrelate with each other to achieve increasingly successful means of communication. Children learn to communicate successfully in a number of ways. They come to understand the functions and purposes of language, they listen intently to the language of others, they develop the ability to interpret and identify the intentions of others, they join in and have a go for themselves. Through experiences of successive approximations towards achieving a working knowledge of their first language/s, they are sensitive to formal language features and they are exposed to the use of language in different contexts. In so doing they become more effective in their own communicative strategies – they usually become effective speech partners before they enter formal schooling. This does not mean that they know all there is to know about language by the age of five or six years. Beyond this time their vocabulary development continues throughout life along with the requirement for more complex grammatical discourse structures, which will be needed to communicate increasingly demanding concepts and ideas to an increasing variety of audiences.

If we knew all there was to know about language then we would also be able to describe this knowledge base to others but we can't. This is because the kind of knowledge we are talking about here is tacit knowledge. We use this kind of knowledge every time we perform automatic actions like speaking and listening, even though we don't know how to describe these actions to others. We have reservoirs of tacit knowledge, which we draw on constantly. When we spend time with infants and young children, however, it is easy to see that they do not have these reservoirs of tacit knowledge and our responsibility is to help them develop these reservoirs. In the context of language learning, we do not do this by giving them lessons in linguistics, but rather by engaging and interacting with them frequently while we use language, spoken and written, for all the purposes we typically use in our daily lives. The most successful parents in this regard are those who treat their young off-spring as equal partners in conversation and other activities from the moment of birth.

Children will build up the tacit knowledge base they require through the feedback they receive from more experienced others. This feedback accepts and praises all their efforts, it also includes modelling, using language appropriately as it is mirrored back, demonstrating while matching actions to words, and importantly giving time and attention to understanding what young children say and write. In these ways they learn that what people (including themselves) say, has significance and importance, that we take turns in listening to each other talking, and that language has meaning and makes sense; and that these meanings can be clarified through further talking and asking questions and can be captured permanently through writing.

Because of the layering of language and its multifaceted nature, children do not learn about language in any additive or linear manner. They learn about all aspects of language all the time they are exposed to it and engaged in its processes. Whatever understandings or knowledge base exist is influenced and altered by new knowledge and fresh understandings. Each developmental increment takes place through a process of incorporation and re-creation, not by a process of simple addition like threading beads on a string. Understanding these notions of processes akin to *assimilation* and *accommodation* is critical for an understanding of developmental processes and helps us in understanding better our interactions with young children.

Awakening and responding to early literacy

Literate adults awaken and support literate behaviours in young children, by providing for literacy 'events' and creating and responding to 'teachable moments'. This is done by using our own knowledge of developing print awareness in children and careful planning, and providing guided activities and opportunities which capitalise on children's individual interests and abilities within contexts that are defined by both purpose and authenticity. Providing purposes for writing and reading that are relevant and supportive of genuine ongoing activities, and are centred in social interaction between adults and children, will create and support connections that make sense to the children between what they already know about print and what is new for them.

Children interact with print during the process of their play if it is made available to them through materials and demonstrations by others around them. Through play, young children encounter and explore their physical, social and cultural worlds and develop strategies for incorporating this learning into their own understandings. For example, in this way children will make lists, labels, 'write' letters and notes and they 'read' these as well as books and other printed material like maps and instructions which surround them and they see others using. They look at magazines, signs and directions, as they become chefs, doctors, pilots, engineers and astronauts, or anything else they imagine through their play. Children's literacy development expands through this natural incorporation of reading and writing into everyday activities which are part of their busy lives as well as of those around them.

This early and expanding literacy development through activity is increased and extensively enhanced towards successful achievement not only through social interaction with another person who is already literate, but through planned interaction. This is what is meant by literacy 'events'. These 'events' are created by the adult as every advantage is taken of children's naturally occurring curiosity about reading and writing in the world that surrounds them. Children naturally ask questions like: 'Show me how to write my name', 'What does that say?' (pointing at a sign) and 'How do you know it says that?' (when adults respond to these questions).

Teachers create and engage children in literacy events that have similar characteristics to those that some parents naturally use in their interaction with young children as they learn to talk. These characteristics include, for instance, providing feedback and encouragement, valuing every attempt, and expecting success and progress. The adult follows the child's lead, answers questions and provides information to link what the child currently knows with new or more detailed concepts than those the child already understands. Teachers do this by pointing out the same piece of information in other circumstances, by drawing the child's attention to similarities and differences: 'It begins with the same letter as your name', 'Can we find that same word in our list by the door?', 'That word sounds just like cat', 'We had that word in our story yesterday, let's see if we can find it printed on the page'. Making responses like these and engaging in the outcomes together; providing feedback and using the language of print (letter, word, page, book, list etc); helping children to use visual *and* auditory strategies; all these enable them to focus on what we do when we read and write and support them in their attempts at literacy behaviours.

'Teachable moments' and authenticity

When teachers act in this way through interaction with children, responding to their inquiries and creating an inquiry where one might have been missed, they are engaging children in what is meant by 'teachable moments'. It is the more knowledgeable adult who takes these opportunities and builds up the expectation in children that help is there when they need it, that the world is a reasonable place even if they haven't found out how it all works or fits together yet. Many commentators on adult-child interactions have described this kind of activity as 'scaffolding'. In reading a story with a repeating phrase, this printed phrase may be pointed out to the children, and then they can be asked to point it out again on the next and following pages. They may need further help and so the phrase can be reread more deliberately and each word pointed to and simultaneously read aloud.

What is happening here is that through sequences of literacy events, supported by teachable moments, children's developing understandings are guided by offering information and gradually putting the responsibility onto the child for identifying similarities and differences in print and for using a variety of visual and auditory strategies for reading and writing with increasing accuracy and fluency. What the teacher does is use language that is not only supportive but also carefully structured. In this way the adult gives each child as much support as they require to solve the problem for themselves, giving minimal cues verbally and therefore illustrating what children must learn to do for themselves. Gradually the gap between what children can do for themselves and what the adult helps them to do will be reduced. Adults scaffold by pointing out and saying words as often as is necessary firstly with the children, then by letting the children read them for themselves and praising their *efforts,*

...comes are successful or not, and enjoying the engage-
...n print together.

These kinds of experiences that expand young children's interest in literacy rather than deliberately teaching them will prepare them well for the relatively more structured contexts of classrooms as they enter primary school. In the preschool, while literacy events may be planned to stimulate and take advantage of teachable moments, they will emerge from the multitude of authentic daily experiences. Experiences from trips and visitors provide opportunities for recording through drawing, dictating and writing for later review and reading. Stories heard aloud provide a template for children's own stories, especially if they are memorable texts because of their phrasing, repetition, rhythm and rhyme.

Activities that imitate adult lives include the appropriate literacies, like taking an order in the café, preparing the menu, distributing bills, counting and recording money. Doctors keep records of their patients and look up treatments in books, they write prescriptions and have labels on their doors. Travellers look at maps and plan journeys, holidays are chosen from travel brochures, special events are marked on the calendar, track is kept of birthdays and lists of favourite games are constantly updated.

What we see here are the two major roles of the adult in children's literacy development: firstly, in providing an environment in which literacy can take place, one in which literacy events are natural and commonplace; secondly, through their carefully guided interactions that take the opportunities provided by these literacy events to engage in teachable moments with children, as their early understandings and curiosity about print develops. These two features of practice will be developed further in the later chapters of this book.

Our main conclusions from the survey of relevant research literature are that:

- systematic and explicit 'instruction' is inappropriate during the early years;

- literacy resources need to be made available for young children to incorporate into their play;

- adult participation and collaboration enhances children's understandings about literacy.

4

Empowering all our children

'I loved these glimpses of a language more alive than mine, words spawning straight from sound waves like single-celled life forms wriggling out of primordial ooze' (Hall, 1997:71). Reflecting on the early literacy experiences of his daughter, Hall encapsulates the wonder of language development in childhood both inside and outside the home.

This chapter explores the extent to which policy makers and practitioners are aware of the key issues surrounding the learning of foreign languages in the early years. Our discussion focuses on adult perceptions of young children and language learning, and is based on research evidence from a doctoral study, data collected for our research projects and from the work of other researchers.

Taking the world as a whole, monolingualism is the exception, yet in several of the richest countries, being bilingual or multilingual is not particularly encouraged, especially when the dominant language is English, for it is assumed that in the near future most people involved in trade will use English. Sadly what is forgotten here is the fact that benefits to the economy are not the only reasons for speaking other languages. And it may be possible to 'buy' using English, but if you want to 'sell' you will make yourself more popular if you speak the language of your potential buyers.

Issues of policy and practice relating to young children from linguistic minority groups, as well as issues relating to the teaching of modern foreign languages in the early years are raised in this chapter under three headings – the child, the practitioner and the policy maker (see also Jago, 2000).

The child

As we observed in Chapter 2, researchers in education have described childhood in terms of social and cultural constructs (Mayall, 1996; James and Prout, 1997; Panter-Brick, 1997). However, new constructions of childhood have been sought in other areas of learning: Higonnet explores the visual history of childhood and questions the portrayal of children in society. In the world of art and photography, she discusses an emerging image of childhood (the 'knowing' child) which 'is difficult in many ways, and confronts adults with many more challenges as well as many more pleasures than any ideas of childhood has done before' (Higonnet, 1998:209). The interface between this art form and literacy education becomes apparent when she turns to the role of the family: 'Thematically, new work about children, which is always implicitly about children's relationships to the adults who photograph them belongs within a much broader photographic revision of family.' (Higonnet, 1998:209). In our own field then, we adults must confront the issues connected with our assumptions about childhood, children's learning and cultural and linguistic difference.

The term 'bilingualism' is not easily defined, yet it is used to describe a diverse range of young children entering the education system:

> it refers to a continuum of linguistic ability, ranging from the receptive bi-lingual who understands a second language without necessarily being able to speak or write it, to the rare ambilingual child who operates in two languages on a daily basis as fluently as native speakers of either language. (Jago, 1999:156)

Children have a remarkable facility to manipulate words and create meanings: sensitive intervention from family members and early years educators can transform the oral articulation of ideas into marks on a page. Drawing upon research into children's patterns of thinking, Nutbrown explores implications for curriculum, assessment and work with parents, and relates these to children's own learning agendas. Exposure to other languages and cultures will not only increase the learning opportunities for all children, but will address the needs of bilingual pupils who can 'develop and discuss their ideas through their home language' (Nutbrown, 1999:68).

Children from linguistic minority groups require learning conditions that encourage meaningful interaction in activities that are sensitive to the home culture.

> Before deciding to intervene and help children from a different language background it is important to determine, first, whether the child is experiencing difficulties in the home language or whether his or her current problems stem principally from unfamiliarity with the new linguistic environment. (Bochner et al, 1997:172)

Marion Whitehead refers to 'successive bilingualism' which usually occurs around the age of three as children become active in the world outside the immediate home environment, and tends to be developed among 'linguistic-minority children when they first attend primary schools, nursery schools, creches and other care centres' (Whitehead, 1997:36). According to Bronfenbrenner's ecology of human development, this stage would correspond to the transition from the microsytem to the mesosystem which 'is formed or extended whenever the developing person moves into a new setting' (Bronfenbrenner, 1979:25).

In their studies of young children starting primary school, both Jo Weinberger (1996) and Hilary Minns (1990) provide insights into the ways in which the cultural and linguistic backgrounds of children from minority ethnic families and communities and their interactions in school and other local contexts are woven, or transformed, into new forms. These children are creating new cultures, drawing on the riches they find in each.

In her highly respected work on what she terms 'emergent bilingualism', Eve Gregory (1996) suggests both an 'Inside-Out' and an 'Outside-In' approach. The 'Inside-Out' approach means:

> recognising children's existing linguistic skills and cultural knowledge (she provides an aide memoire of questions teachers can ask themselves – about the child's home culture and language, older siblings, own teaching approach, other resources in the community, how activities at nursery relate to those experienced at home, mechanisms for gathering all this information);
>
> • building aspects of the child's home and community knowledge into the preschool curriculum;

- limiting the size of a teacher-directed task;

- modelling 'chunks' of oral language during role play or with puppets;

- devising home-school literacy links which will involve both parents and children as mediators of different languages, in ways they will find comfortable and valuing.

In the 'Outside-In' approach the teacher 'bathes' the children in 'the 'magic' that a good story-book holds for all children and then the teacher 'scaffolds' children's early literacy experiences by:

- linking spoken and written language through the use of drama, music, cookery, art etc.;

- defining the rules of class story-reading sessions so that children begin to realise the difference between 'reading words' and 'talk about the text';

- 'modelling' reading and enabling children to repeat manageable 'chunks' of text in chorus first;

- increasing the language demands on the child gradually' (Gregory, 1996:142).

Gregory also emphasises the importance of the socio-dramatic play area but she warns that for young children who are emergent bilinguals it is important to recognise that the teacher and assistants provide the only, 'target language' models. This modelling can be effected by the teacher taking part in role play (which she can extend but should let the children direct or lead) and also by involving proficient native speaking children, or puppets, to help model the language. Setting up the socio-dramatic play area as familiar contexts – such as a café, the newspaper/ sweet shop, the supermarket, which all the children know in the local area – is another key strategy.

Most importantly, early years teachers need to reflect on the devices they use to assess young children's competence. A number of studies show how some children from linguistic minority communities have been underestimated because they were too reserved to show their achieve-ments, or because they could not understand a key word in what was being asked of them. Additionally, teachers need to be sensitive to the kinds of worlds the children inhabit – for some it may be a world of television and computer games, for others the mosque and language classes, for example.

For all children, including those living in monolingual communities and attending monolingual nurseries (where at home all the families use the native language of the country), experiencing and respecting other languages enriches the curriculum. In our research, in England for example, children in one nursery celebrated Chinese New Year and the staff invited a mother who could speak Mandarin to come in and talk to the children about China. She taught the children a song in Mandarin, based on counting to five, showed a clip of video from a children's television programme recorded in Shanghai and used a large toy panda as a puppet who 'could not understand or speak English'. In another nursery (geographically closer to France than to London), the children often ask the staff to count with them in French, after they have counted in English. They sing French nursery rhymes and the displays of their artwork include drawings with simple French words as well as English, together with cuttings from French magazines. On one occasion the cuttings were about babies, part of their current theme about 'growing and changing'.

The practitioner

Storytelling is not only a valuable and enjoyable literacy activity to share with young children, it is also a central issue in the impact of research on policy and practice. 'Policy makers and researchers with different views of the nature, purpose or potential of education and/or teachers tell a different story' (Ozga, 2000:13). Without research that offers different stories, there can be no alternative strategies to those proposed or imposed by central government. Ozga argues that 'the contradictory aims of education and the different things that it does for state and society, place considerable pressures on teachers and make their work and its management complex and unstable' (Ozga, 2000:13).

The Early Literacy Links project has explored with early years educators in England and France their stories and understanding of literacy in all its forms. As we explain in Chapter 5, a complexity of issues and increasing media attention surround literacy experiences in preschool settings, as national strategies and guidelines are developed for young pupils in England. Children possess a multiplicity of literacies which need to be supported and extended at school and in the home but which are not always explicit or readily described in a teaching manual.

When French teachers were asked if they had any anxieties about early literacy teaching, at least two aspects of the impact of socio-economic and cultural factors on literacy development were raised by teachers. First, in the areas of economic and social deprivation in which they work, most of the teachers from whom we gathered information were very aware of their role as the main 'literacy mediators' for some of the children in their class. Some teachers also felt that their work is not always acknowledged and understood by some of the parents from different cultural backgrounds, whom the teachers think perceive the *école maternelle* as a *garderie* (*crèche*). In order to overcome this problem the teachers organise meetings so they can explain the aims of the activities they organise.

French teachers who mentioned bilingualism also emphasise their view that this is likely to have a negative effect on literacy development. Not surprisingly we only observed examples of non-roman script in two of the fifteen schools where we observed. Thus a negative view of bilingualism appears to pervade the French system and this may be taken to reflect two related dimensions of the French context:

- French constitutes an essential aspect of the national identity;

- not many systematic studies of bilingual schoolchildren have been carried out in France. Those which have been published (for instance Blanche-Benveniste *et al.,* 1992) were originally triggered by a negative view of bilingualism. In the light of current research on bilingualism and the different educational policies promoted by different European countries (Tabouret-Keller *et al.,* 1997), it seems that this issue requires further investigation in the French context.

Meanwhile, research carried out by Anning and Edwards in a range of English early years settings examines the perceptions of educators and parents in relation to the acquisition of language and literacy in childhood. 'The practitioners in the project brought with them distinctive preoccupations and discourses about language and literacy from their respective …working traditions as childminders, carers and educators'

(Anning and Edwards, 1999:78). They also assert that sensitive observation and interaction are paramount with children who are already multilingual: it is essential to plan experiences which will scaffold their literacy development. Practitioners will require, for more than one language, a degree of 'knowledge about literacy and a sense of progression in literacy acquisition, achieved through ongoing professional development, dialogue with others and a critical knowledge of research, policy and practice' (Nutbrown, 1999:72).

Equally, planning for learning is crucial for bilingual children in the early years of education but learning must take place in meaningful contexts. Knowing how each child will 'make sense' of the nursery setting depends on staff having a 'learning partnership' with families and communities, where the practitioners are the learners.

In an account of literacy experiences within the preschool environment, Reynolds describes her own professional development. Her comments could equally be attributed to working with children from linguistic minorities.

> It soon became clear that my role as an early childhood educator was not to prepare children for literacy but to accept and extend what children already know about reading and writing. What I had become was a provider, facilitator and nurturer of the children's emerging literacy. (Reynolds, 1997:35)

Exposing children from monolingual or native-speaking families to other languages extends their thinking. We know that during the first year of life babies everywhere (unless there is a physical reason for them being unable to do this) make the sounds used by any language in the world. However, by one year of age the neural connections for the sounds they hear around them, relating to their home language/s, will have strengthened and all others will have 'died out'. It may be that by ensuring children *hear* other languages, even if they do not learn them formally until later, their ability to *speak* other languages will be enhanced.

The policy maker

The value placed on, and government response to, multilingual literacy learners in the preschool setting is crucial not only in terms of the child's self esteem but in recognition of the home background: social and cultural conventions are learned through the medium of language. 'In our society [UK], the same status is not accorded to being bilingual in English and Urdu as to that given to an ability to speak English and French' (Suschitzky and Chapman, 1998:57).

The education of young children is not value-free: research in this context is subject to ethical codes and guidelines, which challenge thinking and practice. Lindsay recommends the development of regional or national bodies to assess research issues. 'Perhaps it is now time to have ethics committees to guide research in education, analogous to those in the health service. These might be formed from representatives of LEA officers, teachers, researchers in higher education and parents' (Lindsay, 2000:20). A similar framework could be applied to the system of education for multilingual learners. Policy makers at the national level must be aware of the different participants in various contexts upon whom the policy-making process has an enormous impact.

The introduction of non-statutory guidance for the teaching of modern foreign languages in England, for children at Key Stage 2 (age seven to eleven) has been a significant step forward in the development of multilingual literacy for young children in England. However, local and regional initiatives for foreign languages in the early years of schooling have yet to be acknowledged. National recognition that young children can also benefit from additional language learning and the kind of opportunities offered to older pupils tends to rest upon issues of funding, staffing and outcomes rather than the innate abilities of very young children to exploit their language learning resources (Jago, 2000).

Campbell has already challenged ideas that no nursery child is ready for literacy. 'Encouraging emergent literacy prepares the children for the literacy demands of later life and equally importantly, helps children come to terms with the print environment in which they live' (Campbell, 1996:62). Through the eyes of a parent, the literacy experience of a three-year-old can offer an image to the policy maker of the enormous power, sensitivity and range of ability that very young children possess and which can be used to foster an awareness of other languages and tolerance of other cultures and literacies. 'Now books could come into their own as windows to the wider world, storehouses of images and ideas that Madeleine could absorb, ponder, tinker with, and reproject onto her own narrower circumstances, lighting them up in new colors' (Hall, 1997:95).

Similarly, Jo Westbrook's (1999) sensitive account of her daughter's early encounters with print and audio-visual images such as videotaped versions of stories, further accentuates the amazing capabilities of babies and young children, when exposed to appropriate literacy experiences. Videotaped and audiotaped stories to accompany texts, story boxes to illustrate traditional stories from many cultures, together with books providing the relevant script for children to follow, are not only essential for the bilingual children and their families; they also provide a way for children from monolingual families to begin to understand how language works and to respect their multilingual playmates.

The researcher

The least a practitioner can do is to treat all the young children in her setting with respect, to make them feel welcome and relaxed by creating a setting which will feel familiar because of the images, scripts and artefacts visible at child level. Further, we have known for around two decades that young children learn and 'perform' best in their first language/s (for example, see Shorrocks, 1992) and it must be remembered that languages which have a rich oral, storying culture do not necessarily have a written form, and that for some the accepted written form is a specific dialect. Children's families and communities are therefore vital partners in the process of understanding what may be meaningful to the young child. Jeni Riley (1999) proposes that effective practice must include attention to admissions policies and to the involvement of families and the communities to which children belong.

For babies and younger children this may mean learning to sing the tunes and songs their families sing to them, using the traditional stories from their cultures, and inviting members of the family and community to spend time in the setting, so scaffolding a 'bridge' for them between the known and the strange new world of which they have become a member.

Work by Caroline Barratt-Pugh (1997) about the ways in which a group of early childhood practitioners were encouraged to remember generalised patterns of development, while at the same time recognising that development can vary from child to child, and to pay attention to the fact that eye contact, gesture, facial expressions, body contact and use of personal space can have different meanings in different cultures. Although some members of her group questioned the dangers of stereotyping as a result of ideas about culturally specific behaviours, they came to realise that above all it was their attitudes and values and, particularly, the ways in which they, the staff, used language which conveyed positive or negative meanings to children. As a result they decided to explore their views on:

- the way language is learned;

- their relationships with the children's families;

- ways of supporting bilingual children;

- how they actually interacted with children;

- whether the activities they provided reflected diversity, enabled children to use language for different purposes, how to help children use more abstract language;

- whether they planned and monitored language;

- and whether their policy on language included literacy.

It is in acting as 'critical friends' that researchers can support practitioners in their search for the most appropriate ways of helping all children to 'make sense' of the print-dependent world they inhabit. They can do this by providing information and by encouraging the educators in their own research, observations and reflections on practice.

Note

1 See Hamers and Blanc 2000 for an extensive and recent review of the findings which emerge from research carried out in education, psychology; neuropsychology, linguistics and sociology and Barrière, in press, for the explosion of research on bilingual development by psychologists, linguists and educators and the theoretical and methodological challenges which research in this area needs to address.

5

Early literacy teaching in four cultures

Influences on provision for early literacy

Preschool teachers' views on literacy impact upon the type of learning experiences they include in their preschool curricula. Even within the four countries we studied, early childhood educators work in many different contexts and this in turn further influences how, or whether, they plan for literacy.

Children's cognitive development, theories of how reading and writing should be taught and issues concerning maturation and readiness for schooling all influence teachers' thinking about literacy education for young children. External pressures such as parental expectations and the policies and curriculum guidelines devised by government agencies all add to the range of issues teachers will take into account in making decisions about early literacy.

In this chapter we contrast our observations and experiences concerning literacy in preschools in Australia, Singapore, France and England. Some of the differences we have observed in the practice adopted by early years teachers reveal differences in cultural understandings about young children and their learning. Differences also arise through the relationships that exist between preschool and school services, and these vary across countries. It is not surprising then to find that many teachers regard literacy as a complex issue. Some teachers would rather leave this topic alone and wait until children go to school whilst other teachers feel compelled to include literacy in their curricula. Many teachers are working under pressure to make greater provision for literacy in response to governments who are calling for higher standards of literacy at school. The uncertainty this creates for some teachers is discussed in this chapter. It is clear that teachers want to know about literacy and young children. However it seems that more needs to be done to help teachers understand how they might develop the literacy teaching and learning in their settings in a manner that is consistent with a child-centred philosophy and pedagogy.

Cross cultural perspectives

Our research in the four countries, Australia, Singapore, France and England, provides some insight into the different views expressed by teachers and the different pressures that they experience with literacy in early childhood education and care settings. In each case the learning experiences that practitioners provided for children were influenced by a range of factors. A role for preschools as preparation for schooling was very evident, although in some settings this preparation was not explicit and practitioners would often emphasise the importance of the 'here and now' nature of young children's experiences. Some even hate the use of the term 'preschool', saying the children are not pre- anything, they are living and learning now. Writing about France, for example, Madeleine Goutard (1993) decried the change in terminology from '*école maternelle*' to '*préprimaire*', saying this indicated a change of philosophy.

Early literacy in an Australian context

In Australia the preschool services are provided through a number of types of settings. The main services are full-time, long daycare and sessional preschools. Preschools are educationally oriented and can be embedded in daycare provision, or in some cases attached to primary schools, as well as being stand alone facilities. Preschools principally provide a programme of educationally oriented experiences for four-year-old children during the year before they start primary school.

In 1996 the Preschool Literacy Project (PLP) was set up in the State of Victoria, Australia. In 1998 a further project called Literacy and Numeracy at Transition (LNAT) was established in schools and preschools in New South Wales. The purpose of the PLP was to investigate preschool teachers' concerns, beliefs and attitude towards the inclusion of literacy in the preschool programme. We also wanted to find out more about the types of literacy experiences that were normally offered in preschools. The LNAT project extended this work and examined how continuity for children's literacy and numeracy learning could be maintained across the boundary between preschool and school.

At this time preschool curriculum guidelines for Victoria emphasised play in indoor and outdoor contexts. Specific issues such as literacy and numeracy were not addressed. Teachers planned for children's early learning experiences based on their observations. This approach was also found in New South Wales. However, more recently, consultations have been taking place to develop a more specific curriculum framework.

In the early stages of the PLP we were struck by the intensity of the response that some of the teachers made when they were invited to participate in this project. A number of teachers were reluctant to engage in research that was designed to consider literacy in relation to preschool age children (four and five years old). Some teachers were adamant that literacy was not the concern of the preschool. When they were asked about their concerns regarding literacy and young children some teachers argued that children should not be 'pushed' into reading and writing too early and that maturation should be allowed to take its course. As a group they were concerned that literacy should not be taught until children went to school. This view led to very limited literacy experiences for the children, perhaps a book corner and one storytime per session but no other activities or resources. In addition these teachers were also worried about parents who encouraged young children to read and write. They believed this to be inappropriate and used the phrase 'pushy parents' to describe parents who encouraged children to read and write at home. These teachers had little concept of literacy (and numeracy) as social and cultural practice within authentic settings, as opposed to formal teaching of reading and writing.

This debate about the inclusion of literacy in the preschool curriculum is not new. It has persisted despite evidence that many preschool children do learn to read and write. A large amount of work has been published describing children's early attempts at reading and writing. It appears that many children are highly motivated to have a go at it. Many parents show an ability to support this development and make provision for literacy experiences at home. Because of this a large number of children begin preschool with an awareness of print in their environment.

Teachers involved in both the Australian projects were able to describe many instances where preschool children showed a motivation to learn about print. Children often asked for the meaning of written information on posters around their room or in books. The children also showed an interest in writing and many children made attempts to produce messages as they noted things down for themselves and others. The form of the print they used was loosely orthographic and often children made a series of simple pencil marks to indicate a message (as discussed in Chapters 2 and 6). Some children were writing down information such as names or putting messages on cards, shopping lists and so on. The teachers also noted that children were showing an interest in books and were beginning to use them to retell stories that were familiar to them. Many teachers were able to identify children who could recite their favourite story and who would do so as the pages of the book were turned.

Teachers also described how the children shared their skills and it was not uncommon to hear a teacher describe how children were teaching each other to write. Children would often spell out names to help a less proficient member of the group. Many children were able to read and write their own name before starting preschool at three years old. They also showed an awareness of familiar signs and slogans and were able to reliably recognise many that were of personal significance to them. Thus during the course of a normal day many teachers observed children participating in numerous literate activities at preschool. We were surprised to find that these teachers did not plan for these experiences and they took very little initiative towards extending them. The children appeared to bring them spontaneously into their play and other areas of the learning.

The Australian teachers also told us about children who did not engage in literacy at preschool. Usually this was explained as being the result of a lack of literacy at home or a lack of developmental readiness of some of the children. The teachers' comments indicated that they saw the home environment as the most significant influence on the emergence of these early literate behaviours. Children who demonstrated a greater awareness of written words were believed to come from homes where talk around print was fostered through the use of books, pencils and paper.

We were interested that these teachers believed that differences in the way children behaved with print reflected the influence of the home environment. However we were puzzled that this insight did not prompt them to develop further scope for children to explore literacy in their preschools. The teachers did not appear to be concerned about children who came from homes where the benefits of rich literacy experiences were absent. They seemed to accept that this would be addressed at school. These teachers did not see a role for the preschool in addressing the early literacy development of such children. They believed that literacy was clearly an issue for school and not a major concern for the preschool.

The confusion created among many of the educators by the idea of introducing literacy into an early years curriculum based on play has been evident in our work in Victoria. Responses to our initial interviews with teachers about the concerns they had about the inclusion of literacy in the preschool programme, showed a high level of apprehension about this topic. The Australian early years teachers explained that their initial training[1] had not directly included literacy development as a curriculum area. Also, they did not know how children became readers and writers, nor did they know how children were taught to read and write at school. They firmly believed literacy to be a skills-based activity that needed to be directly taught through exercises. Consequently, they were concerned that they might adopt inappropriate teaching practices and create problems for children when they went to school. They were concerned about the issue of 'curriculum push-down'. We were surprised at this level of concern and apprehension, as these teachers were also able to tell us about the children in their preschool centres who were beginning to read and write.

Despite their own observations of the interest the children displayed in reading and writing the teachers continued to regard literacy as belonging to the more formal learning environment of school.

Early literacy in Singapore

Preparation for primary school, which children start in the year they turn seven, was particularly evident in Singapore. Here the teachers who participated in our research were working within a system that placed an expectation on the nurseries to prepare children for primary school. Children in Singapore join toddler and infant groups after the age of one year and begin Nursery 1 at age two to three years old. They progress by age through Nursery 2 (three to four years), Kindergarten 1 (four to five years) and Kindergarten 2 (five to six years).

An important component of their curricula was, therefore, to introduce children to the rudiments of written language, along with numeracy and appropriate classroom behaviour. The preschool practitioners in Singapore use workbooks and direct instructional methods to teach children to read and write in two languages in the nursery and kindergarten programme for children aged two though to six years. The children are usually taught in English as well as Chinese, Malay or Tamil.

When children start primary school in Singapore at age seven, they are expected to arrive already able to

- write a 30-or 40-word story, with correct grammar in English, about a personal experience;

- pronounce correctly three-syllable and most four-syllable words

- read simple, five-line stories in picture books;

- express themselves and give answers and directions in English.

Further, Singaporean children are expected to speak 600 words and read 400 words in Mandarin, and to write 200 characters, before starting primary school.

In the preschools we visited, children were grouped together for instruction and then expected to complete set work tasks such as reading a particular page or storybook, or pages of set work in a workbook. The children were also instructed in number and computer skills, the latter in dedicated computer rooms. Consequently the approaches were teacher-directed and the children were given little opportunity for self-directed play in these activities.

However, we were interested to hear the teachers in Singapore express concern about the level of demand being place on children. They questioned whether there was too much pressure on children in the Singaporean system. Further, the children were also assessed on entry to school, so the teachers were also concerned that they might fail at the very beginning of their school careers. These teachers felt unable to change this situation and felt obliged to ensure all the children would leave their centres with the necessary school entry skills. Consequently a large proportion of time in the preschool sessions was devoted to skill mastery in each of the different languages. As the new century begins, however, this heavy emphasis on preparation for school in Singapore is being re-evaluated and fresh guidelines are expected to address the need for moderation in such emphasis on school preparation during the preschool years.

The Early Literacy Links project

Like the Australian projects, the Early Literacy Links (ELL) project has also adopted a cross-cultural approach in order to gain a better understanding of the contexts in which young children become familiar with literacy in France and England. The project was carried out on both sides of the English Channel/*la Manche*, over a two year period from August 1998 to July 2000.

The French context

Some common features characterise the demographic changes which France and the UK have experienced in the last 50 years, namely the immigration of workers from abroad, including people from countries which formed part of their respective colonies. Thus a proportion of children who attend school learn the main language of their country of residence as an additional language. These children are bilingual, or in some cases multilingual. The national language policies which have influenced the educational provisions exhibit some crucial differences (see Tabouret-Keller *et al.,* 1997 for comments on the refusal by France to ratify European linguistic minorities law).[2]

French children aged three, or even two in some schools, are systematically entitled to attend *École maternelle* (*EM*) and more than 95% of the children aged between two-and-a-half and five years old benefit from these provisions. Compulsory education starts when children are six, when they are required to attend *École Élémentaire* (*EE*) (Oberhuemer and Ulich, 1997).

As in the Singaporean context, the transfer between preschool and primary school seems a difficult experience for many children, as the adult-child ratio jumps from 1:10 to 1:40 (see Raban and Ure, 1999a: 47). In order to improve this situation the division of the French primary school career into cycles (each of two to three years) was established in 1991 (*Ministère de l'Education Nationale*, 1991).[3] The aim of the cycles is particularly relevant to the focus of our project: it is to prevent children's failure in the first year of primary school and especially to improve the the low literacy achievement, usually the main reason why children in France must repeat a year of their schooling (Béchennec and Sprenger-Charolles, 1997).

The recent division into cycles is expected to improve children's achievement by:

- allowing more flexibility with respect to the age at which specific skills are to be acquired: a child is allowed an extra year, if need be, to reach the targets set for the end of each cycle by the French Ministry of Education (MEN);

- encouraging a policy of *décloisennement* (decompartmentalisation), to facilitate the transfer between nursery and primary school.

French literacy research

This section briefly outlines the effects which various and sometimes contradictory research trends have had on the content and implementation of the preschool and school programmes. According to Chartier *et al.* (1997), the current foundations of the curriculum are best described as the outcome of the last 20 years of research and have been influenced by Anglo-Saxon approaches to literacy.

Between the First and Second World Wars, a debate took place between those teachers who adopted a *méthode naturelle* (analytic method starting with a global approach) and those who adopted the *méthode mixte* (in which the memorisation of whole words precedes a syllabic approach). In the 1970s, the educational debate surrounding literacy teaching was renewed owing to a number of developments: the influence of linguistics on education; the findings which emerged from research on phonology and which resulted in more rigorous accounts of phoneme-grapheme correspondences in French; and a clearer distinction between oral and written language (Chartier *et al.,* 1997). The official instructions of 1972 and the textbooks published in the subsequent two decades encompass these developments (Hébrard, 1988). Almost at the same time, other domains of research – including new trends in literary criticism, semiology, psycholinguistics and sociolinguistics – altered the perspective on reading, the relationship between reading and writing, and the approaches to literacy teaching (Chartier *et al.,* 1997). Some theoretical models, most of which were influenced by Anglo-Saxon approaches (through translations of the work of Frank Smith) redefined the notion of text comprehension in reading. In France this new approach to comprehension emerged from literary criticism rather than from psycholinguistics and seemed to bring a solution to the failures experienced by some schoolchildren and observed by their teachers. Thus after the publication of the official instructions in 1972, teams of teachers tried to emphasise the construction of meaning and find ways to implement this new approach to comprehension. This led educators to introduce authentic reading material in their classrooms. During the 1980s, new investigations on reading focused on

- the representation of literacy by learners (with the work of researchers such as Downing and Fijalkow (1984) and Fijalkow (1997) which addressed some issues which Ferreiro had first raised);

- the code (see Sprenger-Charolles, 1988; Rieben and Perfetti, 1989);

- eye movements, memorisation and information processing (Chartier *et al.,* 1997; Rieben and Perfetti, 1989).

Although the aims of researchers and teachers are distinct (Fayol, 1997; Chartier *et al.,* 1997), their interactions have triggered the renewal of teachers' initiatives and the revisions of school programmes (see for instance Chauveau *et al.,* 1993; Garcia-Debanc *et al.,* 1996).

It seems that the current French preschool and school curricula have attempted to reflect the sometimes contradictory findings which have emerged from these research projects.

'Entrée dans l'Écrit': early experiences of literacy and the national early childhood curriculum in France

The documents published by the Ministre d'Education Nationale (MEN), which outline the objectives set for each cycle including those on literacy, seem to encompass the multi-faceted nature of literacy discussed for instance in Auzias and de Ajuraguerria (1986) in which the social, cultural, communicative, emotional, linguistic, perceptual and motor aspects of literacy development are integrated.

The publication *La Maîtrise de la langue à l'école* (MEN, 1992) provides a list of the objectives set for each cycle and suggestions as to how to reach them. In addition, it also includes a summary of the current research on literacy development and a selective bibliography. An essential aspect of literacy development emphasised in the preface by Lang, Minister of Education at the time, is that literacy activities are to be *enjoyed* by children.

The rich perspectives on language and literacy development presented in the national curriculum (MEN, 1991, 1992) are:

- Entering literacy
  - exploring writing and reading material in context
  - becoming familiar with books and newspapers
  - listening to stories being read
  - formulating hypotheses on actual experiences and on situations evoked/represented
  - formulating hypotheses on textual situations.

- Learning to write
  - talking, to tell (stories) and to explain
  - dictating to an adult
  - writing texts.

- Knowing the code
  - listening to language and observing written material
  - making progress in graphomotricity
  - learning to write
  - learning to spell.

- Being able to read
  - reading with the help of an adult
  - reading alone.

(Based on Chartier et al., 1997:23)

During the nursery stage the teachers are expected to immerse the children in the spoken and written language, using both cursive writing and print in their displays in order to develop a love of the French language. However, most of the activities are provided to foster children's 'discovering, awakening, becoming sensitive, growing awareness'. The notion referred to as *éveiller* (awakening) is often used in the French literature on early childhood. Generally the children are regarded as 'working on' the above activities rather than achieving proficiency. So before they are formally instructed how to read and write, young children are to be familiarised with various types of activities and material involving literacy and encouraged to improve various aspects of their oral language skills, in order to prepare them for using these in later reading and writing.

Several features of the French approach are similar to that of *Emergent Literacy,* identified by Goodman (1986) but which has not been translated into French (Chartier *et al.,* 1997). These approaches to early literacy involve engaging the children in discussion on or about:

- discourse characteristics of written language;

- printed material in context;

- metacognitive and metalinguistic awareness about writing;

- the use of oral language to talk about written material;

- the forms and functions of literacy.

    (Nutbrown, 1997)

Although they evolved in different socio-cultural contexts and educational systems and constitute the outcome of different research trends, the notions of *Entrée dans l'Écrit* and *Emergent Literacy* have much in common, in content at least.

However, it is in the interpretation that they differ, since, like the teachers in Singapore, these educators used group instructional teaching methods and worksheet type tasks to introduce children to French language concepts. Teaching plans were predictable and the teachers were able to indicate in detail what they would be teaching in the next week, next month and so on.

This skills-based approach was also consistent with the curriculum the children would encounter when they progressed into primary school and the teachers felt their young pupils would be competent in what would be expected of them on entry to the next phase of their education. Thus the French teachers did not feel a need to consider alternative approaches to literacy. They were convinced that the approach adopted in France would ensure that all children would have the prerequisite skills for reading and writing at school. One teacher voiced her opinion that the children succeeded because they were instructed in what they needed to know.

However, despite the visible structure and whole-group sessions in the French nurseries, a high proportion of the French teachers told us that they worked to ensure that young children enjoy literacy activities and that they understand the functions of literacy. Some suggested that the graphic work undertaken by children prepares them for writing. Only about one in eight of the practitioners told us they thought children assign a meaning to the material they read or write.

Most felt that the targets set for each cycle by their Ministry were attainable and did not cause them concern. Perhaps because of their long education and training, the French teachers were calm and confident about their approaches and their ability to help the majority of children in their nursery classes to achieve the targets. While they reported that they did not feel that their views were overtly and formally taken into account by the MEN, changes made were in line with their informal feedback. In particular, the French teachers were content that the sections of the national literacy document prescribed for the nurseries were suggestions and targets, rather than a rigid programme. This means that the French preschool teachers were free to teach creatively in order to implement the curriculum.

Unlike their Australian counterparts (Raban and Ure, 2000), all the French preschool teachers we asked thought they should encourage literacy development in children.

So the kind of activities they told us they provided include:

• story-telling and discussion; the use of the book corner/school library/other libraries (in practice this was, typically, fairly restricted and controlled by the teachers);

- the use of a variety of reading material; graphic activities (often worksheets);

- showing children the functions of literacy (for example, cookery recipes, letters);

- visual discrimination;

- the use of various writing tools and support;

- relating literacy to children's own experiences (such as 'signing in'/ finding one's own name on arrival); encouraging activities involving the family;

- writing and receiving letters.

We subsequently observed all these activities in action. However, we observed that in many cases the story-telling sessions in *écoles maternelles* also involved teacher behaviour patterns which would have helped young children gain insights into the working of printed material, and which the teachers did not mention to us, such as:

- the teacher reading a story to children while showing pictures and/or pointing to the text;

- the teacher asking children to carry on a story (sometimes with the help of the pictures);

- children being asked to provide an appropriate title for the story they have heard;

- children being asked to recognize the printed title of a book;

- children being asked to describe a story based on pictures;

- children being asked to draw appropriate illustrations for a story they had composed.

Very few teachers mentioned tasks focusing on the small units of literacy such as word-level recognition and phoneme – grapheme correspondence. However the storytelling sessions observed often involved peripheral activities during which children were sometimes asked to recognise some words or to establish a correspondence between a grapheme and a phoneme. As David notes, such findings demonstrate that

> in many ways French early years teachers behave in much the same ways as the effective English [primary phase] teachers of literacy, drawing children's attention coincidentally to features and functions of literacy during story telling sessions for example, as described by Medwell et al. (1998) in their report to the TTA (Teacher Training Agency). (David, 1999:8)

Although most of the early literacy sessions observed in France were teacher-led, it appeared that the children engaged in the literacy activities without coercion, understood what was expected from them and showed high levels of concentration.

The French nurseries also had 'ritual literacy activities', which seemed to signal the beginning of the school day. Once all children were in class and their parents had left, they would, for example, name and recognise the label for the day of the week and any current festival, sort out the weather chart, and count aloud the number of children present.

The *Cahiers de Correspondance* (home-school notebooks), in which French children write or stick messages to be signed by their parents, and the *Cahiers de Vie*, which inform parents of the activities carried out in class (such as the songs and poems they have been learning) and in which parents are encouraged to insert pictures relating to the child's home life, were the main literacy activities involving the family. A few teachers mentioned additional ways to establish home-school links such as asking children and parents to cut out pictures and words from magazines, to illustrate a specific sound. We also saw exciting ideas, such as posters about local events at child height in the book corner – posters with clear print and repetition of the name of the town in which they live. One showed a painting of a local park and building, announcing the town's poetry festival.

As if to emphasise the French belief that in the *écoles maternelles* the aim is to *immerse* the children in language as a preparation for formal reading and writing instruction in the primary school, the majority of those teaching children aged two to four did not think their pupils ready to learn how to read and write. However, half the teachers of the four- to five-year-olds in the *écoles maternelles* did think their pupils ready, although the other half did not, and almost all the teachers of six-year-olds said children in that age group are ready.

Thus we concluded that the French approach is consistent with the view that literacy must be taught rather than co-constructed, yet speaking, reading and writing in French are of paramount importance as aspects of 'being French'. The teachers stated that the primary role of the *École maternelle* is to prepare children for school and society and it is in this statement that we begin to see how French children are seen as citizens from the moment of birth. Being a citizen means one has certain entitlements, or obligations – depending on one's point of view. One entitlement of a French citizen is being enabled to use the French language effectively and lovingly, enjoying literacy.

The English context

During the last twelve years there have been major changes in primary education in England and in the last five, to nursery provision. To detail all the changes here would probably take up the whole book, so we will only explain briefly about the main initiatives impacting on the early literacy experiences of children of five. The advent of the first ever English National Curriculum and national assessments, on entry to school (called Baseline Assessment) and at age seven, have influenced preschool practice, even though these were not directly intended to involve the nursery sector (see for example Sylva *et al.,* 1992). In 1996 the Government of the day gave recognition to the importance of the earliest years, by providing funding to all group settings offering places to four-year-olds, as long as they could show, through the newly inaugurated education inspection system, that their curricula would enable children to reach the 'Desirable Learning Outcomes' (SCAA, 1996) on entry to the reception class of primary school. A heavy weighting is attached to aspects of literacy in both the inspection system drawn from the Desirable Outcomes and the Baseline Assessment tasks.

When the National Literacy Strategy (NLS) was set in place by the New Labour Government in 1998, teachers of Year R (reception class in primary schools for children aged four to five years) were expected to use the strategy like their colleagues teaching older pupils, but to use the timings of the different activities flexibly, since for older children the session was to last an hour each day. Recent research (Clark, 2000) shows that there has been growing formality and teacher-led didactic exposition in early years classrooms which can be attributable to the

NLS. Further, despite Government advisors stressing the need for imaginative teaching of the Literacy Strategy in Year R, there are many stories of headteachers and school inspectors exerting their power over early years teachers and insisting that the NLS be achieved through hourly blocks of formal activity. So although this initiative was not applicable to nurseries, it has inevitably influenced preschool practice because early years educators fear the children will be unable to sit still, work independently on literacy-related tasks, and hold a pencil 'appropriately' (a comment frequently found in the under-fives' sections of primary school inspection reports, David and Nurse, 1999), unless they have some practice in these behaviours.

Following much lobbying by early years groups and feedback on consultation concerning revised Desirable Learning Outcomes, now called Early Learning Goals (QCA, 1999), the situation appears much more favourable for young children. The reasons for this are that the Early Learning Goals (ELGs) are intended to be achieved through play (whereas the earlier document for England did not mention play in connection with learning). Working parties developing guidelines for practitioners (QCA, 2000) have included representatives from both the National Literacy Strategy and the National Numeracy Strategy and it is reported they are content that the Early Learning Goals will form a firm foundation for children's literacy and numeracy learning in their later educational careers. Another very important feature of the advent of the Early Learning Goals is that they apply until the end of the Reception Year (that is, until children complete the school year in which they become five). So the message is unequivocal that both the National Curriculum and the National Literacy Strategy begin in Year 1 of primary school, the year when children will become six – more in line with many other countries' (particularly European partner countries') policies about the beginning of 'formal' schooling.

As the Early Learning Goals only become applicable in September 2000, the preschool practitioners who participated in our research in England were still subject to inspections based on the Desirable Outcomes. However, our findings provide a way forward which is even more important in the light of the emphasis given in the new ELGs to play.

Early literacy learning in English early years settings

Perhaps the most fascinating finding from the English research has been the approximately fifty-fifty split among the teachers in views about literacy. Around a half of our questionnaire respondents said children should not be expected to be involved in literacy activities until after they reached the age of five, that they should be allowed their 'childhood' and to learn through play. The other 'half' said that the children would be surrounded by literacy from the moment of birth and that most of them would therefore be learning about it anyway.

Following this, our observations revealed some interesting contradictions. In some of the settings which were assertive about their emphasis on play, rather than on using play as the vehicle for literacy and ensuring meaningful connections between play episodes and reading and writing, children were called away from play to sit with an adult either singly or in small groups, to carry out a set task which was totally unrelated to what they had been doing at other times during the session. The prevalence of this approach has been confirmed by advisory teachers and others in positions to have such an overview in many other areas of England.

Meanwhile, in other settings the whole learning experience would be carefully orchestrated so that children could use the book corner, wall-charts (such as the alphabet frieze, class list, calendar and posters), together with the writing equipment made available, and incorporate these into their play. Both groups of respondents agreed that play should form the basis of early learning and both seek to adopt practices in accord with their avowed child-centred philosophy, so why do some resort to very formal, unrelated adult-imposed tasks when they need to fulfil the requirements for literacy?

Some of the teachers in England, like their Australian counterparts, showed more uncertainty regarding the inclusion of literacy in their programme. While some suggested that readiness for school emerged with maturation, the main reason they gave for engaging the children in these formal literacy encounters was their fear of the Ofsted (Office for Standards in Education) inspections and what they understood to be the expectations of such inspectors.

Environments for learning

The different approaches taken by the teachers in these four countries was also evident to us through the appearance and the design of their preschool classrooms. For instance, the classrooms in England and Australia were designed to facilitate play and as such there were characteristic areas such as the home corner and block corner, sand box, dressing-up clothes and so on. Tables were set up with a selection of activities from which children could choose for a significant proportion of the time during sessions. Puzzles, creative art experiences and materials such as play dough, scissors, paper and pencils were readily available for children. There were displays of children's spontaneous artwork around the room. While these elements were also evident in the settings in Singapore and France, their centres also contained more classroom areas for storage of workbooks and the tabletops tended to be cleared and arranged for children to sit and work on teacher-directed tasks. In England, France and Singapore there were wallcharts such as numbers, the alphabet, and information about learning topics such as the weather, food, plants and animals. In France the displays also included many examples of teachers' writing in print and cursive script (in France children are taught cursive script from a very early age on the basis of physiological theory). These displays could be lists of the children's names, recipes, lists of days of the week, words related to a current theme, and so on. Again, such evidence accords with the expectation that a nursery teacher will 'bathe' the children in both written and spoken French.

Developing learning communities

What is emerging from our projects is first and foremost the commitment of the early years teachers in all four countries. Their care for and about the children is paramount and they work hard, many of them with very little in terms of resources, or in inadequate premises where they must pack away the equipment every day if the building has multiple use. At present, apart from the French teachers and some English teachers, the dedication of early childhood professionals is rewarded with pitifully poor pay and conditions.

Secondly, we have become aware of the need for support in accessing recent research findings and time to reflect with colleagues about the applicability of those findings to their teaching and to children's learning. Additionally, early childhood educators need networks, which will help them make information about the research and appropriate early learning experiences available to parents and policy-makers.

In other words, there is a need to develop 'learning communities'. Such communities are most likely to be localised or regional, but nowadays there is no reason why there should not be 'virtual communities', where early years teachers share ideas and concerns across national and language barriers. For in being challenged by the assumptions and practices held in another society relating to early childhood, young children's learning and literacy, we may begin to 'see' the implications for our own.

Notes

1   See chapter 1 for information about the differences between the education and training of the practitioners in each of the four countries, and the age of admission to primary schools.

2   The ELL project aimed to investigate literacy provisions for young children in areas of economic and social deprivation. Thus the area chosen in England was formerly a thriving industrial community, now experiencing severe levels of unemployment, and the French area selected exhibited similar socio-economic characteristics. The project team was very graciously welcomed and assisted by the French National Education Inspector in an area which used to be prosperous but which has experienced a period of socio-economic decline. It is also characterised by a high percentage of unemployment, particularly affecting a significant proportion of young people (more than 13 per cent of the 16–24 age-band); the lowest average income in the country and, compared to the national school population, the proportion of immigrant children among the pupils in preschool settings and primary school is relatively high (between 4 and 8 per cent) (Ministère de l'Education Nationale, de la Recherche et de la Technologie, 1998). Thus, not surprisingly, a high proportion of schools benefit from ZEP (Educational Priority Area) status (between 16 and 24 per cent) (Ministère de l'Education Nationale, de la Recherche et de la Technologie, 1998). Despite these obvious disadvantages, this part of France also exhibits: a) a very low proportion of school delay and a fairly high rate of success at the baccalauréat (French A level) – between 63 and 67 per cent – which has dramatically increased since 1975 (more than 37 per cent) (Ministère de l'Education Nationale, de la Recherche et de la Technologie, 1998).

3   The French system of cycles and classes

Cycles	Content	Class Division	Age Range
1	First learning experiences	E.M – 1st and 2nd and beginning of the 3rd Year (GS)	2-5 (to 6 if needed)
2	Fundamental learning experiences	E.M – 3rd/Last Year (GS)	5-7
		E.E- 1st (CP) and 2nd Year (CE1)	(to 8 if needed)
3	Consolidation	E.P – 3rd to 5th Year	8-11
		(CE2, CM1, CM2)	(to 12 if needed)

4.   It is important to beware of making generalisations based on our relatively small questionnaire and interview samples from one area of France. However, we checked our findings for authenticity with teachers and inspectors from other areas and, like the preschool practitioners in Tobin *et al.*'s (1989) study, they agreed that our comments characterised their system.

5.   Group settings in England attended by four-year-olds are mainly reception classes of primary schools, and younger four-year-olds may attend nursery schools and classes attached to maintained (public) schools and private schools, day nurseries, integrated nursery centres offering edu-care, and preschools (playgroups).

6

Play approaches to early literacy learning

Paving the way

'I love you Dad'. This message is pinned up on the notice board in the manager's office of a small bank in an Australian country town. A proud dad displays his son's first writing for their world to see (Fig. 1). His son is spending his last preschool year attending the sessional kindergarten in the town, a kindergarten where the teacher and her assistant are keenly introducing their children to literacy through many avenues provided by the children's natural curiosity and their play opportunities. This teacher knows that the children will be taught to read and write when they start school and she feels free, therefore, to take the time to introduce these children to stories and other books of all kinds, as well as literacy materials in all their various forms. She is not alone. Many preschool teachers enjoy the surprise and interest even very young children show when they are introduced to literacy materials. In the Preschool Literacy Project in Victoria, Australia, some 40 preschools and childcare centres

Figure 1

joined together to explore the many ways in which they could firstly create a literate environment for their children, secondly give reading and writing a purpose, thirdly create an awareness of the conventions of print in its many different forms, and fourthly investigate their own role in encouraging and supporting literate behaviours.

Creating a literate environment

These teachers' first concern was the room that the children entered each time they attended the kindergarten. In Victoria, kindergartens provide sessional preschool provision for three- and four-year-old children. The teachers involved in our project looked carefully at any writing displayed on the walls and made sure that where possible this printed material was placed in the children's eye-line. They looked critically at the book corner and began to invest in more picture books of high quality. They placed the books attractively in front-cover-forward positions and in one instance got help to attach plastic guttering to the walls so that books could be displayed for a variety of purposes around the room. (As an aside, in one English nursery the teacher in the ELL study had made copies of the front covers of currently used books, so that children could find where they should replace each book on their similar display.) There were quiet and comfortable areas for books to be browsed through and other areas where books could be studied closely because of the informative photographs or diagrams. Books invaded every area of the room.

Appropriately chosen titles were displayed near the fish tank, for instance. Audio tapes and accompanying books were banded together at the listening post, books with numbers in the stories like *The Very Hungry Caterpillar* (Carle, 1969) were displayed with other number equipment, similarly *The Bad-Tempered Ladybird* (Carle, 1982) was displayed near the clock faces, for example. Map books, catalogues and magazines were made available. Storybooks were placed by the dolls' beds in the home corner for bedtime story reading, and DIY books were included near the construction area. 'Big' books were purchased (or borrowed from the primary school) for story-time/read-aloud sessions and props were made so that children could re-enact their favourite stories. ✳ These props included finger and hand puppets, felt pieces, photocopied characters mounted on card, coloured and laminated, dressing-up clothes, story sequence cards and the like.

An important addition to their rooms was the writing table. This was a popular idea gleaned from Reynolds' book (1997), a book these teachers found very accessible, being written by a Victorian kindergarten teacher with similar concerns to themselves. They noted in the journals they kept that this table evolved over time as the children expressed interest in different resources. Paper of all colours, shapes and sizes was made available along with forms, envelopes (not used), and headed notepaper made up on the computer (with the children). Pens, pencils, and writing tools of all kinds were placed in easy reach of the children. As with books, writing materials invaded every area of the room. There were clip-boards with pencils on string, there was a post-box, a suitably stocked table in the reception area inviting parents to write a letter to their child, and writing materials and books outside the room to provide children with opportunities to incorporate literacy into their outdoor games.

In the home corner, materials were displayed to support the activities that were taking place. For instance, recipe books were placed by the cooker, there was a calendar pinned to the wall, magazines and catalogues were stacked, the telephone had a telephone directory and notepad with a pen, diaries were available, and forms for placing orders, and paper for lists and records of various kinds as the children's play evolved into hospital dramas, shopping, police duties and other imaginative experiences they chose.

Giving reading and writing a purpose

An important aspect of this introduction of literacy into the preschool was to enable young children to develop a conceptual framework for literacy before they started school. This conceptual framework would support these children to understand better and respond more appropriately to the formal teaching of reading and writing that would occur at school. This conceptual development would be particularly important for those children who experienced little literacy in their home environments, or who did not experience the literacy of schooling very frequently. For instance, bedtime stories, writing shopping lists and cards, following recipes, looking up TV programmes, all give young children a sense of the purposes for reading and writing. While surrounded by print in our everyday lives, some children may not have its significance pointed out, they may not have more knowledgeable others pointing out the links between what is spoken and what is written. These children will be particularly vulnerable without some form of support and encouragement to explore printed materials during their preschool years.

Writing of particular salience for all young children is their own name and that of others. This provided the starting point for many activities. Some teachers provided a signing-in book (Fig 2.) for the children (as well as the parents), another provided a 'borrowing list' for a favourite book. Children were encouraged to write their own names on their work and their name cards were made available for them on the writing table and other suitable places around the room. Some children took great care in practising writing their names and those of their family members (Figs. 3). Andrew made his name from the letters he found in a magazine (Fig. 4). Setha said she couldn't write her name when invited to, but she was successful four months later (Figs. 5 and 6). Carley wrote the word 'school', her name, telephone number and address (Fig. 7). She was especially pleased to write her house number 206208 (twenty-six/twenty-eight). Hayden at four years and ten months was keen to show how many numbers he knew (Fig. 8) and Rikki happily identified herself with the written form of her name (Fig. 9).

These requests to write their names were spontaneous in some cases and encouraged in others. Whatever words children asked for were written for them to look at, copy, or incorporate into their imaginative play. When a birthday party was planned, invitations were prepared and 'posted' in the letterbox. Name cards were prepared for the table and suitable cake recipes were investigated. Lists were made of the number of children coming to the party and further lists were required of the favourite games to be played.

What was happening for these children was the opportunity to incorporate literacy into their activities in an ecologically valid manner. While their teachers would suggest writing things down, making notices, recording experiences, sending messages and the like, the children quickly followed this lead and incorporated literacy quite naturally and effectively into their play. Cards were a popular choice of keeping in touch, especially at Christmas time (Fig. 10) and a 'get well' card for a friend (Fig. 11) was designed without any assistance. This was initiated

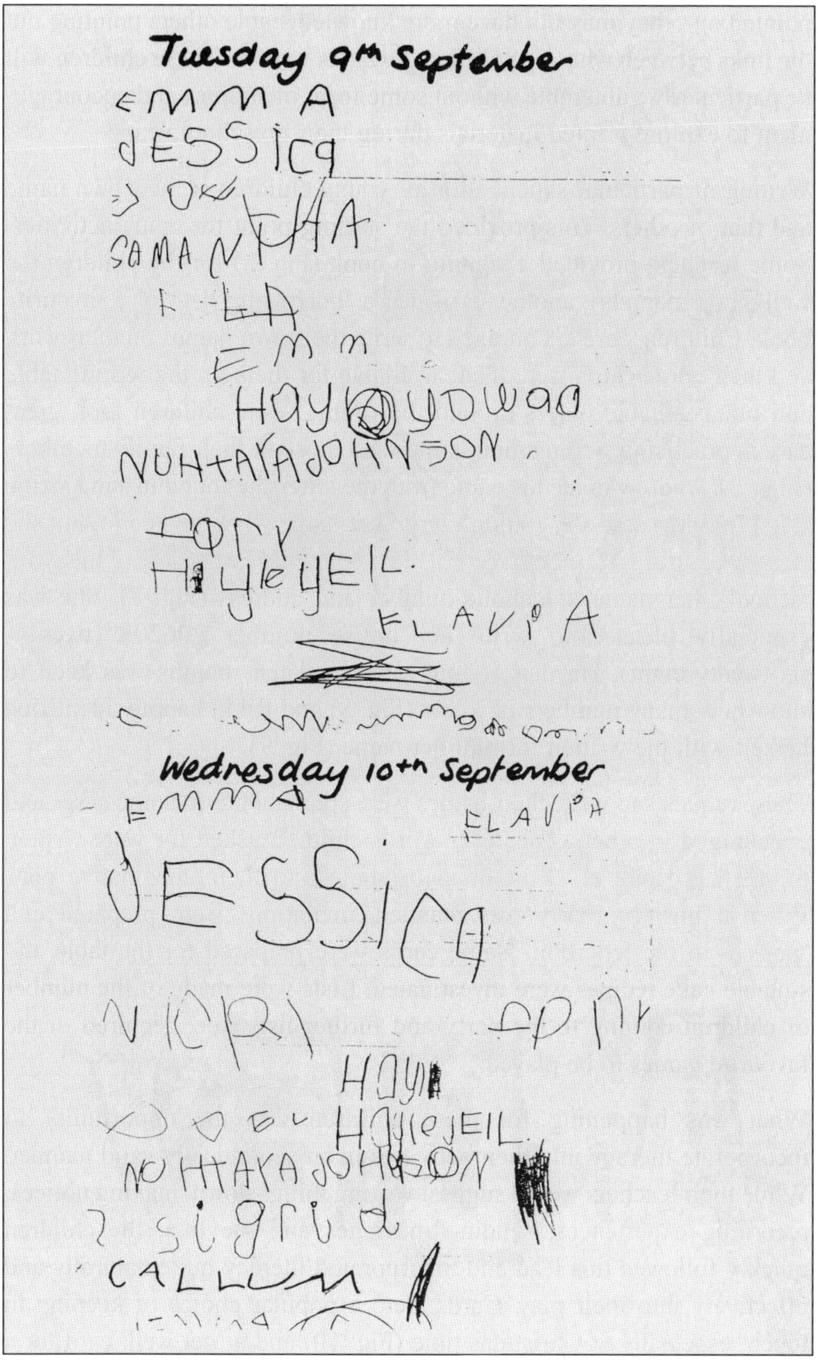
Tuesday 9th September
EMMA
dESSica
FLAVIA
Wednesday 10th September
EMMA
FLAVIA
JESSICA
sigrid
CALLUM

Figure 2

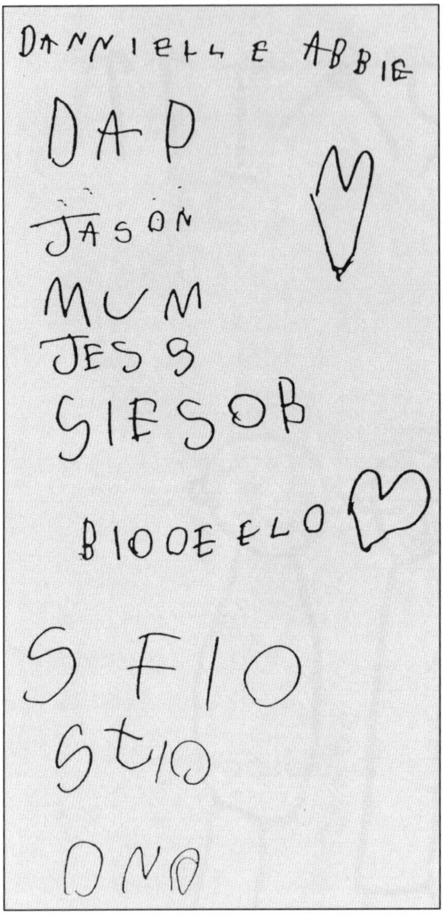

Figure 3

Figure 4

Figure 5

Figure 6

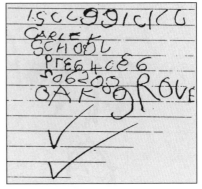

Figure 7

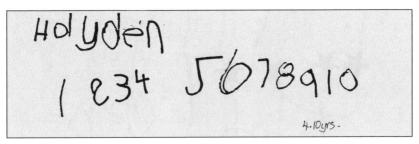

Figure 8

Figure 9

Figure 10

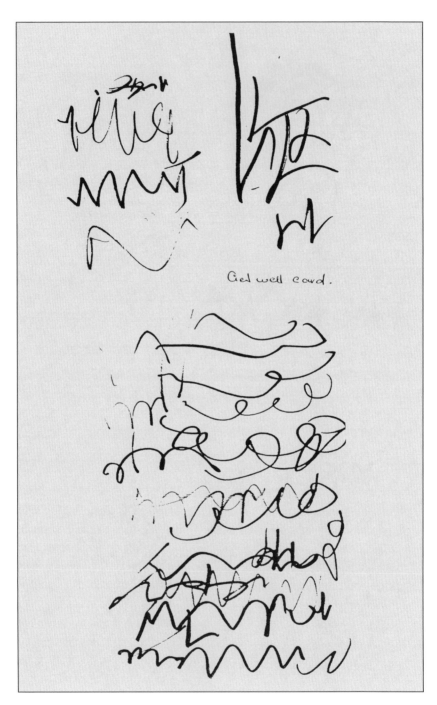

Figure 11

by the teacher, who always remembered to send a card for each child's birthday and for other important celebrations. Post-cards were sent from holiday resorts, and at mail time the teacher shared with the children cards she received from her own friends.

Teachers also generated curiosity around receiving and sending letters. One teacher took the group to the post office, she had cut out pictures for the children to post in envelopes that parents had addressed for them. When they got to the post office; they each queued for a stamp and posted the envelopes to themselves in the letterbox, ably assisted by the staff. They were then treated to a visit 'behind the scenes' and all the sorting and stacking procedures were explained to them. Their teacher took photographs and when they returned to their kindergarten a 'book' about their visit to the post office was created with those children who were interested. As this was where the action was for some considerable time, all the children wanted to contribute something. The home corner became the post office for a while and children were delighted when 'their' picture arrived in the mailbox at home.

The post office featured in many play activities and soon a post-box became a feature of the room. Letters were written and posted each day with a special time for delivery. Everyone wanted to know who would get letters and what was written. When the children wrote letters to each other, but were not yet writing recognisably, they used photographs of each other to stand for the 'to' and 'from' places (Fig. 12). Sophie's letter to her teacher and the assistant (Fig. 13) was in reply to their letter addressing some of her concerns about a bus trip that had been arranged. Sue and Kath also received a letter from Ana (Fig. 14) expressing what she would miss when she was away from them. Contrasting this with Erin's letter to her teacher (Fig. 15) makes clear the range of observable skill among children during this year before they start school. However, they all displayed an awareness of the purpose and function of reading and writing and this was what these teachers were keen to foster. Ben was not observed to express any obvious curiosity where print was concerned, however he took his turn when no one was around and wrote a note to his mum (Fig. 16). His teacher was not even aware that he could write his own name, but given the resources, the opportunity and demonstrations, he felt confident to reveal his undoubted skill.

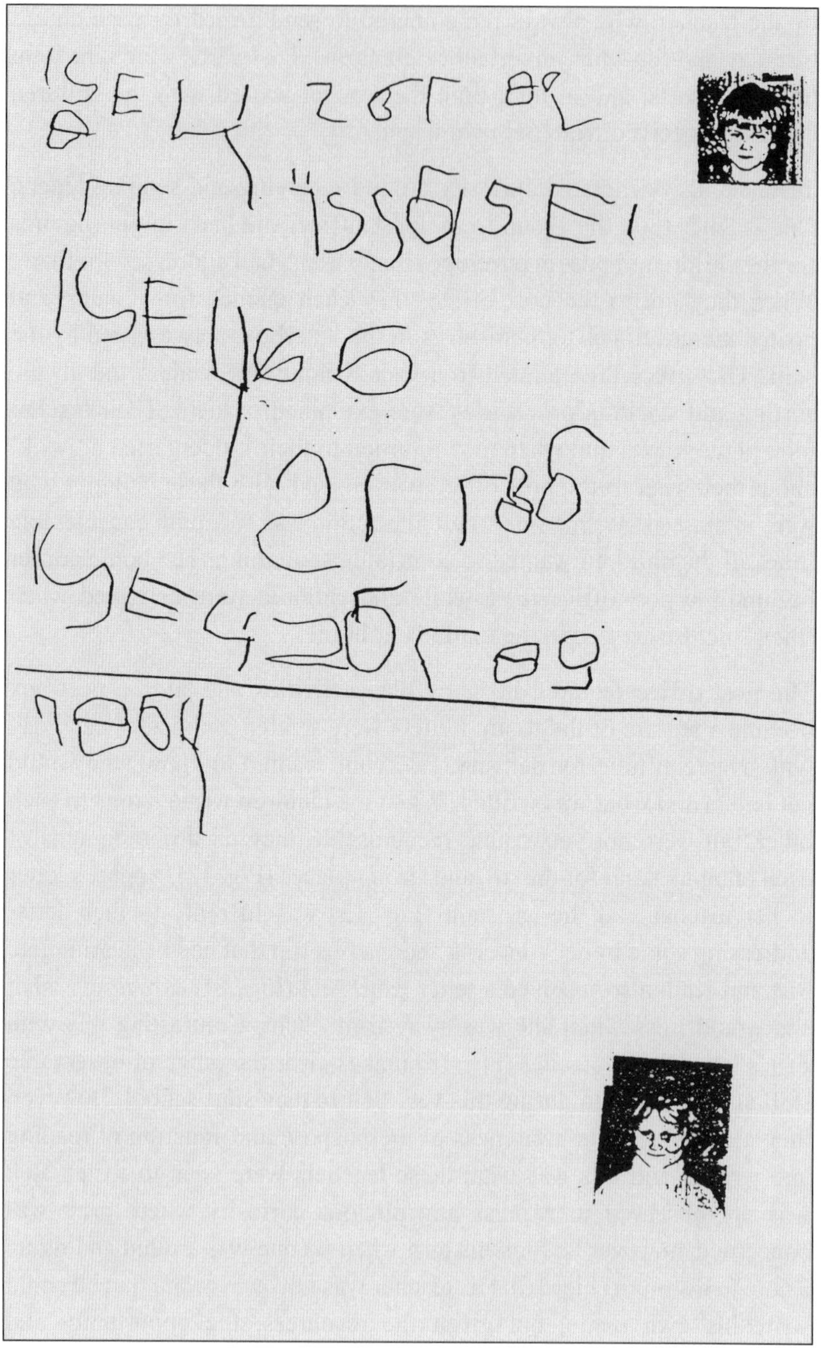

Figure 12

Figure 13

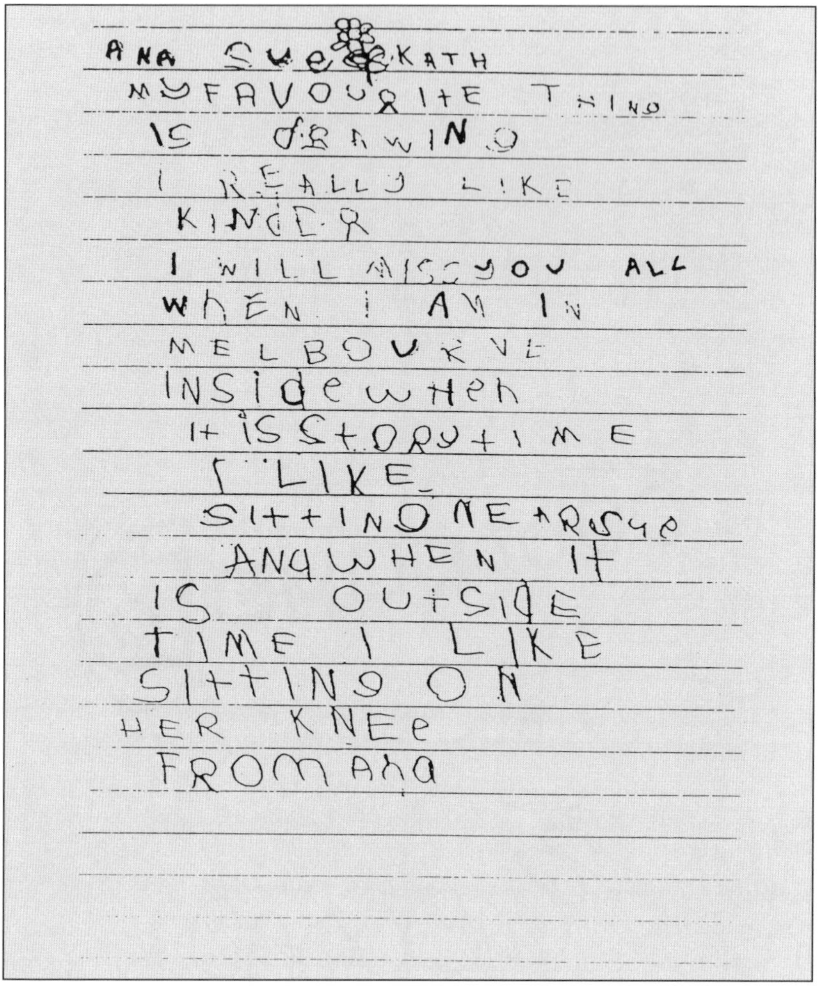

ANA SUE KATH
MY FAVOURITE THING
IS DRAWING
I REALLY LIKE
KINDER
I WILL MISS YOU ALL
WHEN I AM IN
MELBOURNE
INSIDE WHEN
IT IS STORYTIME
I LIKE
SITTING NEAR SUE
AND WHEN IT
IS OUTSIDE
TIME I LIKE
SITTING ON
HER KNEE
FROM ANA

Figure 14

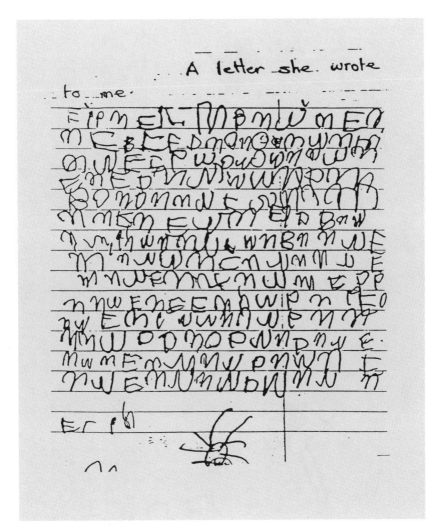

Figure 15

Figure 16

Children were keen to share their sense of good behaviour with their teachers, and notices were placed where everyone could see them (Fig. 17). The children drew each other's attention to these notices and made some up of their own. The teacher placed notices round the room to attract children's attention. They would see something new and want to know all about it. Signs round the room would also be in several languages and children were fascinated by this, copying the words for themselves (Fig. 18) and putting their list on the wall beside the original posters.

Placing literacy materials around the room and engaging with children in their play, making notices, making a reminder note, jotting a message for example, was a powerfully suggestive means of encouraging children to do the same. In the block area, not known usually for its role in literacy development, Nick was puzzling how to make pieces for a board game he had invented and managed to display his ideas in a plan (Fig. 19). Matthew demonstrated his ability to think in three dimensions through his drawing of a cube (Fig. 20). The home corner with dress-ups provided all manner of real-life experiences that gave rise to expressions of related literacy activity, for instance menu cards when it was a restaurant, lists of lay-by items when it became a shop (Fig. 21), and records for the police station and the hospital. Magazines in the 'waiting room' also provided interest as typefaces and coloured letters added to the children's developing curiosity. They were keen to point out the letters in their name; also to find letters that looked different but were the same (D and d) and those that looked the same but were different (f and t) (Fig. 22). One child, in her personal exploration of, and play with, the 'e-ness' of e, took home her 'story of e' (Fig. 23) as she called it, only to return the next day and go straight to the painting area (Fig. 24), demonstrating convincingly that the concept of this letter was now secure for her.

Creating an awareness of the conventions of books and print

Children's drawings and paintings are a rich source of their stories and other imaginings. Some children are keen to share these with their teacher and converting these stories into writing will give children a sense of how spoken language can be captured by writing and how these

Figure 17

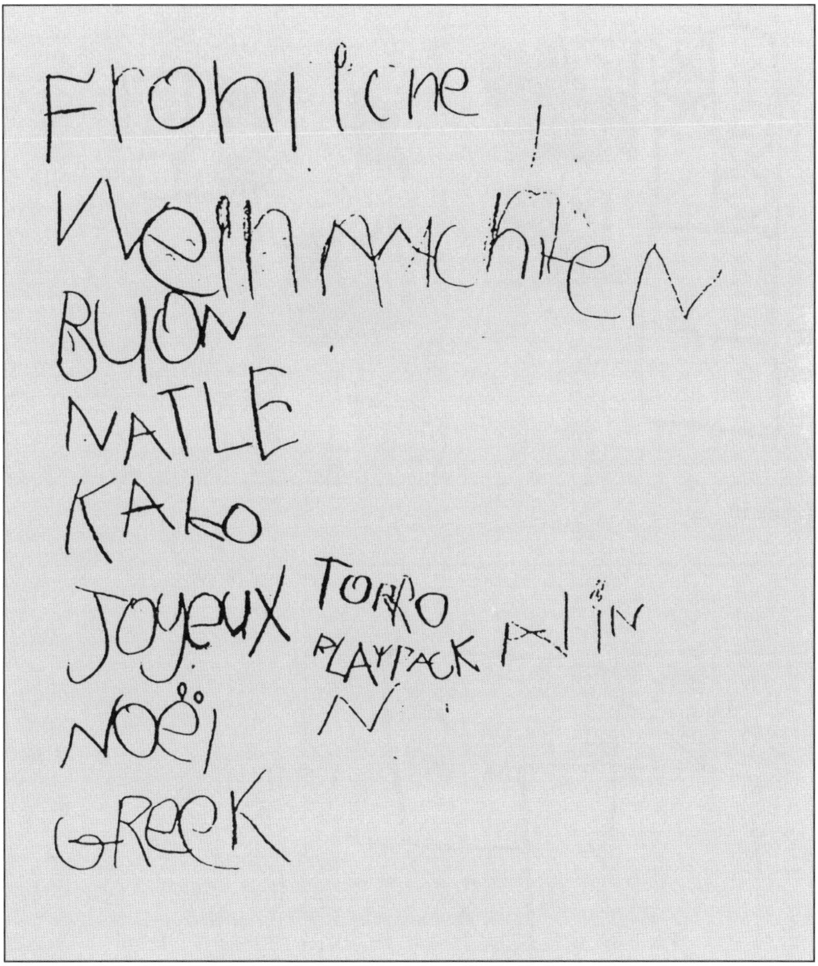

Figure 18

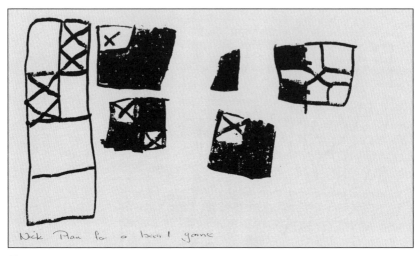

Figure 19

Figure 20

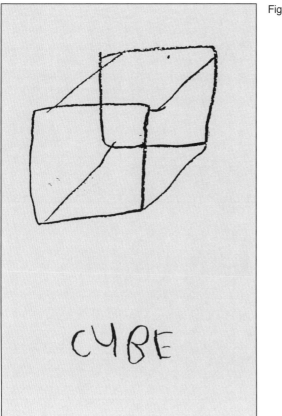

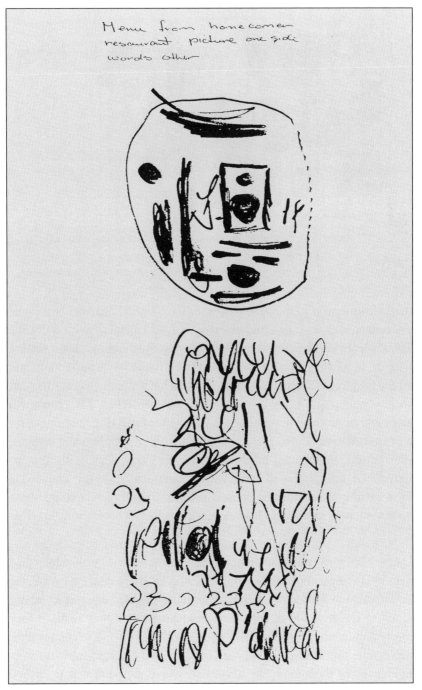

Figure 21

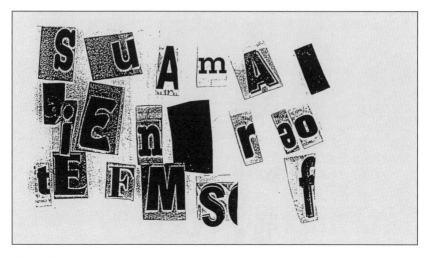

Figure 22

marks can lend a permanency to what they say. These will be crucial understandings that all children need before engaging with a formal literacy learning programme. In addition, the child can watch the writing happen. In writing English, we start at the left and move to the right and sweep back for the next line. Some children have already worked this out for themselves and enjoy demonstrating their skill (Fig. 25), others will rely on their teachers to produce the writing for them (Fig. 26). Pages for a home-made book also provide children with information about pages, illustrations, sequences of events and the like. This will also be introduced through shared book reading, but transferring this knowledge to something the child can join in with adds to the understandings about books and how they work. Some pages from Brett's book show this (Fig. 27).

Using books as ways of entering imaginations is a well-established activity in preschool programmes. However, these teachers took the opportunity to inspect closely how they used books. They read stories aloud to children and talked about the pictures, but they realised they rarely pointed to the print as they read. Thinking of ways to engage children's attention with the book-ness of the activity started some teachers talking about the author, the illustrator, where the book was published

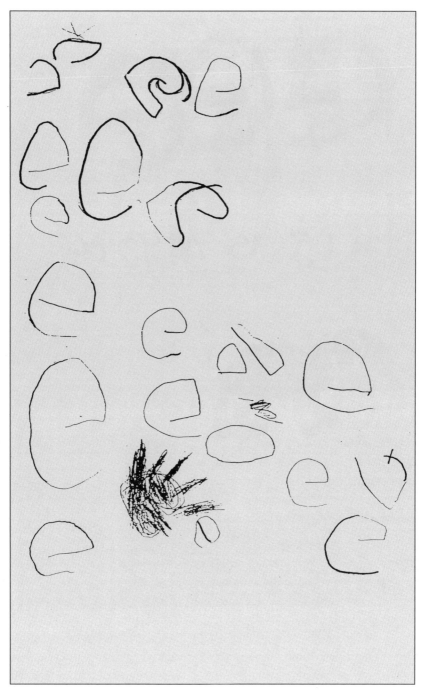

Figure 23

Figure 24

Figure 25

Figure 26

Figure 27

and printed, page numbers, indexes and lists of contents. Soon they found the children begin to do this for themselves in their own play activities at the writing table.

Drawing children into the imaginary world of story saw one teacher engaging the interest of her children in a tale that the children could perpetuate and finish for themselves. She wrote out *Hush's Story* with the children, a story about a possum:

Hush and Grandma Poss have just returned from a trip round Australia.
(This part involved lots of referring to a map book)
They ate Mornay and Minties in Melbourne,
Anzac biscuits in Adelaide,
Steak and salad in Sydney,
Pumpkin scones in Brisbane,
A Vegemite sandwich in Darwin,
Pavlova in Perth,
And a Lamington in Hobart.
(Favourite foods fuelled much discussion here)
They met cousins in Tasmania, Hush 1 and Hush 2, who decided to return to Bendigo for a visit.
(Lots of talk about cousins at this bit)
Grandma Poss arrived home to find she had lost her glasses and has to return to all the cities they visited to try and find them.
(Counts of who wears glasses, whose grandma wears glasses etc.)
She cannot leave them alone so she has asked the children and their families at our kindergarten to care for her precious possums, Hush 1, 2 and 3.
(Why can't she leave them on their own?)
They are to keep a special diary so she can enjoy the fun they have while she is away.

DIARY INSTRUCTIONS

Ask someone to help you write about your adventures. You can draw pictures and take photographs for adding later. Please keep this diary in a safe place (out of reach of toddlers) and return Hush and diary during your next session.

CARE OF POSSUM

Due to over-eating on the journey around Australia, they do not need real food until Christmas. (Pretend food is OK). Possums do not like water and become very scared when handled roughly.

We hope you enjoy your special visitor, and we look forward to hearing about your adventures.

INSTRUCTIONS
HOW TO CARE FOR POSSUMS

Your child has been selected to care for Hush 2 until their next kinder-garten session. Please help your child record in the diary provided their adventures. This can be done by writing, drawing, or even photos. Please feel free to be creative.

Please ensure that all Hush's belongings are returned and if you would like to add any extras they would be most welcome.

PS. THESE POSSUMS ARE ALLERGIC TO WATER / FRUIT / MUD / TOOTHPASTE. They only eat pretend food.

This extended activity engaged children and their families in introducing children to literacy through dramatic and other play activities. Parents sewed tails on the puppets, took them on outings, helped them choose TV programmes, and generally entered into the spirit of this imaginative adventure. This teacher valued the way in which families joined in with their children and through this was able to share with them the basis of her work in fostering the children's interest in reading and writing generally.

Parents donated items for the writing table: forms from their work place, catalogues of cars and farm vehicles, order forms for buying things and business cards etc. The writing table was always a popular choice for the children and they took time there to 'have a go' for themselves and to try out writing. They would make lists (Fig. 28) and write in letter-like forms (Figs 29 and 30) asking their teacher to 'read' what they had 'written'. They would endlessly copy alphabets and numbers from charts on the notice board in their 'office' (Fig. 31) and make notes in the

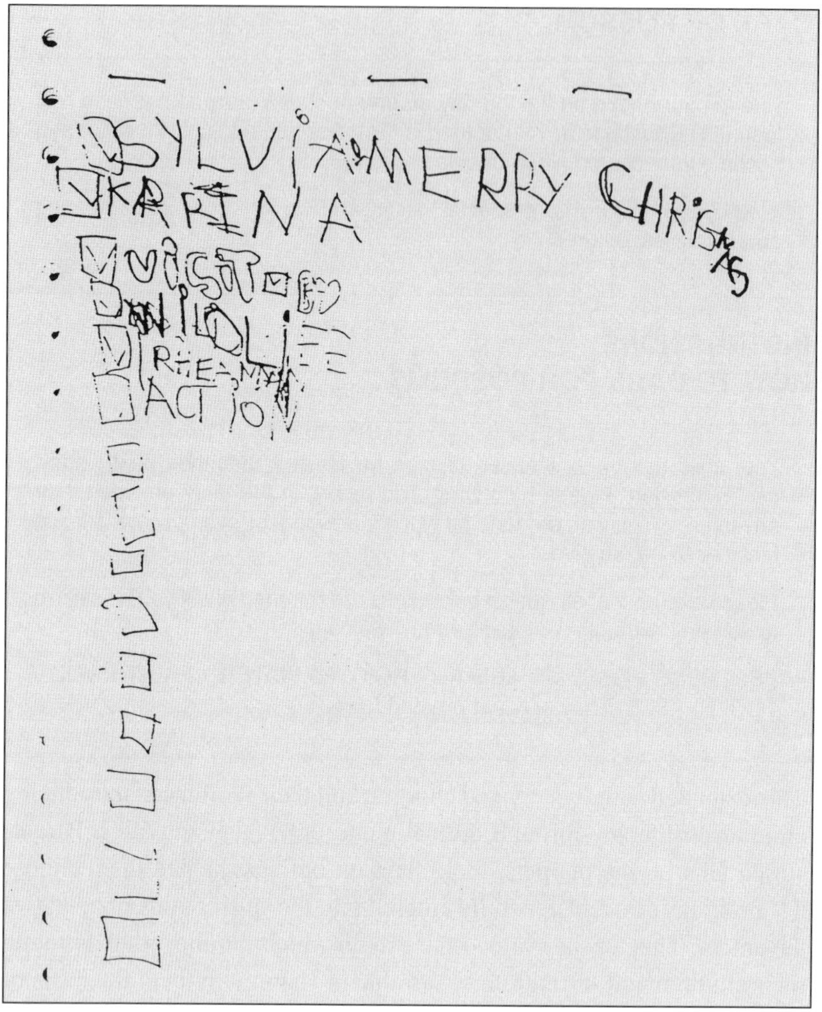

Figure 28

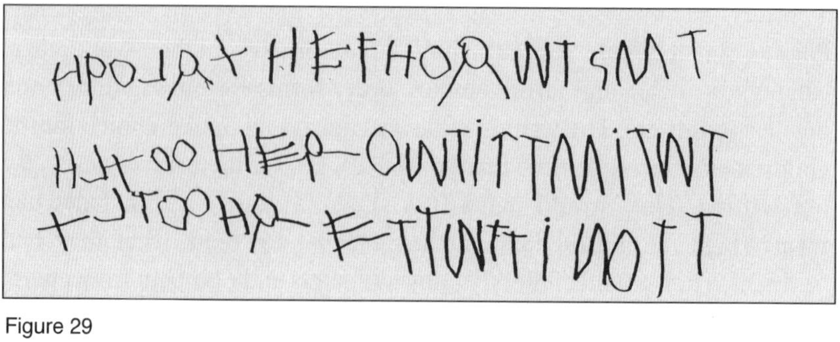

Figure 29

Sam sSamantna
1 2 3 45 6 7 8 9 10
ABCDEFGHIJKLMNOPQRST
UVWXYS

lOIB hGm

Figure 30

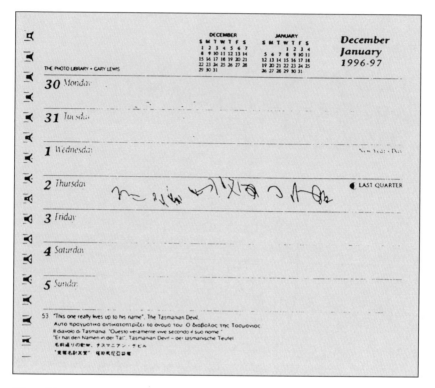

Figure 31

diaries that littered the telephone table and the 'desk' (Fig. 32). The noticeboard was also a place where new information could be pinned up. For instance, when one child had a baby sister and this was reported in the local newspaper, that item of news was cut out and pinned to the board. Towards the end of the year the teacher wrote out the addresses of the primary schools each child would be joining and the children were encouraged to write a letter to their new school. One child was stapling pieces of paper together for days before he presented them to his teacher saying that he had made a log book for his dad to keep in his truck.

Literacy embedded in experience

What these teachers learned was that their children's literacy development was forging ahead on all fronts. Different children approached literacy in different ways and accorded it different values. Some were utilitarian in their uses of literacy, others placed literacy into their

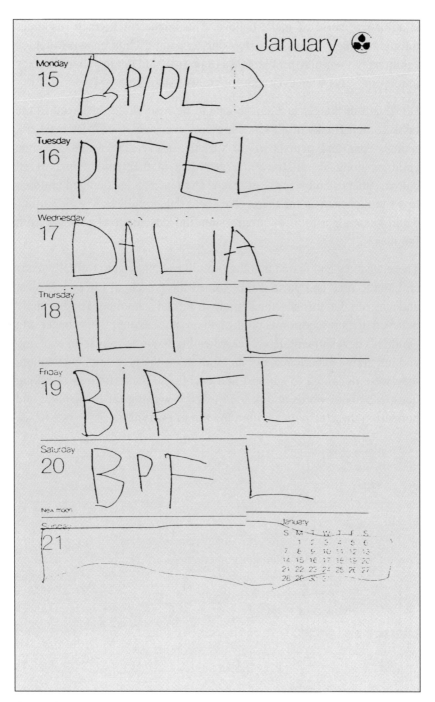

Figure 32

imaginative world of make-believe. The impact of literacy resources throughout their rooms was step one, engaging children with literacy solutions to their play problems was step two, and talking about literacy in relevant ways whenever appropriate was step three.

Books are no longer just storybooks to be read aloud or placed in the book corner. Books of all kinds are now everywhere in these teachers' rooms. Pens and pencils of all varieties are easily available to the children alongside all the other activities in the room. Paper of all colours, shapes and sizes is in reach. The teachers encouraged children to write their names for themselves, and dated children's work so they could keep a portfolio of progression and development to share with families.

These teachers had feared that they would be called on to formally teach children to read and write if they joined the Preschool Literacy Project and they felt that this was the domain of formal schooling. They strongly believed that preschool was predicated on other assumptions concerning children's development. However, when literacy was seen as an evolving and integrated experience, not an 'add-on' to the preschool curriculum, they were delighted to support and encourage their children in asking questions about words and printed texts, in writing for themselves and honouring these activities within the fun of everyday.

7
Literacy events and teachable moments

There is no one beginning, no single system of entry into literacy.
So what, learned early, makes a difference.? (Meek, 1991:97)

'The beginning is everything' (Plato)

Understanding beginnings

It should be an exciting time in schools. In the UK and Australia the current governments have long decided that education must be prioritised duing their terms of office; the Literacy Strategy in the UK and the National Goals for Schooling in Australia are seriously underway in most schools; and how literacy should be taught is indeed the core of many if not most educational conversations. However, in the UK it seems that literacy has been tied down in classrooms and placed securely now into timed boxes to meet the spurious needs of agencies who believe that they have discovered the way to raise standards in literacy, despite the informed views of experts in the field (Whitehead, 1999; Graham, 1999; Meek, 1998). As always it seems in education, a top-down (what the Americans call 'push-down') approach is the result, if not the intention, of new initiatives, and consequently the reverberation of the Literacy Strategy is now being felt in preschool education.

At the same time, it continues to be important to be able to deconstruct not only what counts as literacy but what constitutes 'reading', particularly as this is now a major part of the political agenda in any discussion of education policy. Psychologists, developmental psychologists, psycholinguists, teachers, parents and politicians struggle to achieve consensus in this. At its most diluted, there are those who define reading as decoding, limiting it only to 'item knowledge' (discussed by Clay,

1998, and by Raban and Ure, 2000); others refer to the construction of meaning. Kress is rather more thorough and more critical in his definition:

> Reading is not simply the assimilation of meaning, the absorption or acquisition of meaning as the result of a straightforward act of decoding. Reading is a transformative action in which the reader makes sense of the signs provided to her or to him within a frame of reference of their own experience, and guided by their interest at the point of reading. (Kress, 1997:58)

This is not to say that making sense of literacy in culturally bound contexts means we will become unable to decontextualise, quite the contrary – in societies where there is a long tradition of literacy, the ability to decontextualise is in fact increased, so we can understand others better and empower children to do so through literacy and perhaps through the communicative avenues literacy opens for them. So this transformative action and making sense is enormously useful in ascribing status to early literacy experiences, for example the significance of environmental print in young children's lives, which may in simple terms be the identification of a shampoo bottle or a toothpaste tube on the shelf in the bathroom. We know that very young children are active participants in a range of literacy experiences in safe and familiar contexts before formal instruction begins.

However, it is becoming increasingly important, as we strive to know more about how children think and learn, to know the nature of such successful engagements with literacy, that is, what are young literacy learners actually doing in these encounters or 'literacy events'? One of the observational tools Marie Clay has developed to assess very young children's competence is the now much used CAP (Concepts About Print) task. The initial question she set herself in devising this was 'What is the child attending to?' (Clay, 1998). She also significantly acknowledges that the kind of knowledge the task assesses about print is only one part of the story. Information of the range of other knowledge children have is much more troublesome to investigate and record simply.

The complexity of children's early cognitive development is now part of our common understanding as early educators. Also, if as Mary Hilton tells us 'cognition is encultured' (Hilton, 1996), then it is vital we gather evidence about early stages in literacy learning to clarify, in her terms, the 'myths and realities' of this. Understanding of the culture of child-hood, home cultures, street cultures, play cultures, must combine with that of the culture of classrooms, village halls and the range of early years settings, to contribute to our knowledge of how young children become literate now in our society.

In this debate of how children learn to be literate it is important to remember that young children do not only learn by being taught by direct instruction. Life in primary schools would become remarkably straightforward if such tempting causal links could be easily proved. Learning does not often happen instantly as a result of teaching, but may result after many meaningful experiences, observations and interactions (Geekie *et al.,* 1999). Indeed, some of these may occur before or outside school: at home, at play, with family, with other children or alone. Vygotsky's (1986) theory helps us further with this idea by explaining that development and instruction have different 'rhythms', although they may be closely connected.

In the following description, an observation of a literacy interaction (a 'literacy event'), the 'rhythms' of development and instruction are both evident as they combine in the children's learned roles as instructor and learner.

> Heather was sitting alone with a mini-version of the text Not Now Bernard. She was engrossed as she re-enacted the story, frequently saying 'ouch' and waving a hurt finger, a part of the story that she had remembered. She had won the book after a squabble with a friend and now she relished the prize by reading and retelling the story again and again. Charlotte walked by, pulling behind her a pram crammed full of dolls and bedding. She paused, noticed Heather and, before it could be predicted, snatched the book and told Heather in a casual tone that she would read it to her. She let go of the pram and retold the story, page by page, complete with intonation, her body moving to the tune of the refrain. Charlotte only occasionally halted to re-establish her ownership of the pram and its contents as well as the book and the connected event. Heather did not flinch as the book was grabbed from her but instead relaxed into the role of audience for Charlotte and attentively received the reading of the story, often looking into Charlotte's face and sometimes scanning the page if it was waved close enough to her. During the period of the reading they were almost completely

unaware of their surroundings – the noise and business of a lively room full of very young children engaged in a range of activities. Their concentration was total, although Charlotte appeared almost nonchalant in her manner. The story ended and at the same time the earlier competitor for the book arrived on the scene with a big book of the same story. They all descended on this text as Rachel balanced it on her lap for a shared reading ... The two girls are three years and a few months old and had been at nursery for just a few weeks. The whole episode lasted for almost twenty minutes.

'Literacy events' of this kind occur almost constantly with different individuals, pairings and groups of children throughout the day and in different play contexts in the nursery. Sometimes the books are stashed in the pram and taken to the courtyard for a reading; sometimes the books appear on the bed in the role-play area, or in the middle of the blocks stacked on a table top, or in the back of a truck; sometimes they are plonked on the lap or in the hands of an adult; often they are carried from place to place as prized possessions without being referred to at all. Core concerns for researchers into early literacy development lie in defining the concept of 'literacy event' and equally in defining the status of such events in the developing process of becoming a reader.

These books, story texts, form a major part of each child's daily agenda as they fight over them, re-enact them, retell the story or simply 'own' them. Meek reminds us that children intellectually explore the nature of their own situations, their own childhoods, in their versions of stories (Meek, 1998).

It is important to give credit to the 'author' of the nursery setting that provides such rich opportunities for very young children to engage seriously with such texts. They do not, after all, happen accidentally but as a result of careful planning – of time, resources and support. It is possible to create 'optimum literacy conditions for young children' (Whitehead, 1999) and in her detailed analysis of the current national and international state of the field of early years education, in terms of politics and pragmatics, Tricia David reminds us that

relationships take time to develop and classrooms are, like the home, places [where] relationships are negotiated and refined...Essentially teaching is about relationships... the relationships between children, about setting up a learning environment, a climate for learning, and this requires know-

ledge of children generally and the immediate group of children in particular.
(David, 1999:1)

Indeed, the finely tuned skills of early years practitioners have long been acclaimed and the sophisticated levels of observation, record keeping and planning necessary to support young children cannot be overestimated (Wood and Attfield, 1996; Nutbrown, 1999).

Layers of learning and teaching

Despite the apparent simplicity in play and conversation in early years education, there are essentially many operational layers in action, often simultaneously. For example, the construction of an appropriate literate environment; the creation and nurturing of relationships between adults and children; careful resourcing; and sensitive interactions and interventions from informed educators. As she reflects critically on how children become literate through a diversity of input and experience, Marie Clay discusses the importance of 'awareness' in young children: awareness of how a story goes, awareness of how a book is organised and awareness of what we do as we read (metacognition). The demonstration of such awareness, she argues, is seen in our interactions with young children and the ways the children use further opportunities for learning created for them by insightful practitioners (Clay, 1998).

The observation described above took place in a UK nursery where such developing awareness is aroused, explored and made explicit to groups of children in shared reading and writing activities using big books and small versions, magnetic characters, names and letters and a variety of story props. These more formal literacy encounters take place daily or twice daily and involve all adults and children in the nursery, giving status to story and talk. The importance of adult modelling and the crucial participation by young learners has been the focus of much recent research (for example, Medwell *et al.,* 1998) and has been prescribed as a major feature of the Literacy Hour in UK schools (DfEE, 1998). Clearly evident in observations of children engaged in book activities and book play is the close resemblance between the teacher-led occasions and the child-led events. For example, during one observation:

> Jane and four other three-year-old girls were sitting on the carpeted block in a quiet room of the nursery. They all held clipboards and pens and were

calling registers, at different times, in different ways and with different 'voices'. Marks were made on their papers and at various stages one of the children almost sang the words 'She's not here, she must be poorly,' until it became a refrain used by all the children in their roles as nursery leaders. One child, Jane, left the group to collect a book, Owl Babies. She held the book in front of her chest, facing 'her class', and retold the story, looking up at regular intervals and using her finger to point at the words and the pictures over the top of the book. She then proceeded to collect other books she 'knew' to read in the same manner.

These events were, in part, a mimicry of the adults the children had witnessed engaged in the same activities. These are not unique events. They happen frequently in playful settings around the globe, but it remains important to signify such interactions and to critically define their importance. The research findings of Vygotsky (1986) validate occasions like this. He acknowledges the levels of learning involved and asserts that in order to be able to imitate it is necessary to possess a way of stepping from something one already knows to something new and different.

By observing and tracking children involved in literacy interactions or 'events' it is possible to establish how important informality and the child-led nature of the occasion is in confirming or reaffirming what information children are gathering about literacy from periods of instruction, teacher-led activities, or simply from their developing life experience.

Imitative behaviour is, as already stated, one important area of development but even beyond this there is evidence that children are doing rather more than simply mimicking. They are engaged in a process of constructing meaning for themselves through their textual interactions and discourse. Before and outside of school, this is evident in children's subversion of texts and their playful risk-taking as they interact with family and friends in word play, humour and audacious irreverence by taking known texts and reinventing them (Grainger and Goouch, 1999). Indeed Chukovsky claims that it is only through playing with ideas consciously and demonstrating their knowledge of sense that they can delight in nonsense (Chukovsky, 1963).

The term 'literacy event' is helpful in describing young children's encounters with reading and writing in a play-based context. It offers the possibility of a window on an activity that can encompass a range of intentions and skills, an activity that is important enough to be described as an event. Kress's (1997) earlier definition helps in giving status to the interaction between Heather and Charlotte described earlier in this chapter. It is the transformative nature of the event that is significant in this context, as both children have succeeded in constructing their own interpretations of the story, signifying the importance of the hurt finger and indeed the refrain in their terms. Both appear extremely satisfied by the outcome and are content that they have read the book. They go on to share their construction with others who then overlay their own experience and understanding on Charlotte's readings. It is also important to note that this particular text is likely to resonate with most children's own experience of invisibility in the eyes of busy parents and with having an overwhelming sense of injustice (although interestingly it is the drama of the hurt finger that remains the core of the memory of this reading event for Heather).

Tizard and Hughes (1984) characterise young children as 'puzzlers'. Certainly the questions they ask of others during shared book occasions demonstrate this, and indeed their own delight in achieving their self-determined achievements is constantly in evidence. It seems that if their interest is aroused, as Kress says above 'at the point of reading', then they are able to sustain interest and co-construct an interpretative understanding that is satisfactory to them.

The children observed in this UK nursery context were seen to be deeply involved in their texts and the interactions related to them and they were allowed uninterrupted time to work at resolving their own intentions, with the story and the event. This deep level of play requires effective communicative action and is clearly both self-motivating and self-perpetuating as their affective responses urge them on to repeat satisfying experiences. It is the originality and creativity of young children's responses that offer surprises to their observers and this continues to be a persuasive argument against simply providing children with a 'handy toolkit' of skills (Hilton, 1996).

The following example is further evidence of how a child uses experience of the power of written language to support his reinterpretation of a strong adult message. Only a few minutes were involved but the level of prior learning evident was clearly demonstrated in this literacy event.

> Charlie, a three-year-old in the same nursery, without obvious literacy tendencies, listened with his peers as their teacher drew a chalk line across the yard and said that bikes and 'wheely' toys are not allowed beyond the line. He responded by taking the chalk and retracing the line with added 'wiggles'. He told his teacher that 'This says you can't bring your bikes over'.

Geekie *et al.* (1999) remind us that 'successful learners' always go beyond what they have been taught. In Charlie's case, categorising play and respecting boundaries and others was the limit of the presented learning. Charlie, however, constructed his own literacy event. His creation of a sign that will affect the behaviour of others is empowering and has grown from both his life experience and his knowledge of texts. In this nursery, Charlie is safe in his interpretative activity and his esteem as a writer visibly grew as a result of this event.

The social nature of learning, the knowledge that learning is most effective when in the company of interested others, has now long been absorbed into the understanding of informed educators working with young children (Bruner, 1986; Vygotsky, 1978). In their analyses of children's literacy development, Geekie *et al* (1999) describe findings from their Australian research: 'Learning in R's class was social and collaborative and involved the joint negotiation of meanings through conversational exchanges. To promote learning the teacher involved the children in collective thinking and joint decision making in the context of literacy activities' (Geekie *et al.*, 1999:216). These researchers maintain that competence in 'referential communication' is essential in school, to facilitate learning. They add that it is possible for very young children to negotiate meaning and collect information from 'more knowledgeable others', if their teachers attend to the lessons offered by research into young children at home with parents and carers (e.g. Wells, 1986).

Literacy events

In the early stages of education children need little encouragement to engage in conversational exchanges. Indeed Charlie, Rachel, Charlotte, Heather and Jane, whom we observed, were willing participants in all literacy engagements and did not need to be 'coerced' into literacy (Whitehead, 1999a). The safety of such contexts and their success as settings for continuous learning to take place, story by story, is dependent on the unending skill and energies of adults, tirelessly interacting to help shape experiences and enable young children to take control of their stories, and thus their worlds.

Defining literacy events with young children is a complex task. Watching and listening to Jane and James helped:

> Jane and James helped each other find rucksacks in the role play area. They put them on and matching black hats and said they were going to school. They didn't have any lunch though. A passing adult advised them to go shopping first and gave them a clipboard each to make a shopping list. They found carrier bags they liked the look of and set off...all the time chatting to each other or a nursery worker, constructing the story, instructing each other. Earlier, following the reading of Bear Hunt, they had also been on a bear hunt together – with rucksacks and black hats!

Journeying became the essence of Jane and James's co-constructed stories. They were becoming powerful authors of their own nursery lives. The construction of informal, child-led contexts is a serious requirement as we acknowledge the continuous, minute-by-minute cognitive development that occurs as a result of the range of interactions possible at this stage of learning.

Nursery contexts and other early years settings provide ideal opportunities for children to engage together in playful language and literacy experiences, to take their word-play, their knowledge of story and their understanding from life, to try out new combinations – their *transformations* – in safe places.

8

Making sense in a print-rich world

The benefits of an early start

Children who enter school with an awareness of print around them have higher success rates in the early stages of learning to read and write. Research about literacy suggests that early experiences with print create long-term benefits for children. Early exposure to literacy at home appears to provide a foundation for later literacy development. Some researchers have suggested that these early home experiences help children develop an understanding about the nature and purpose of print. It appears that children who have had these early home experiences are more able to make sense of the literacy experiences and expectations of primary school. They arrive at school knowing about print as a medium for exchange of information and they understand the processes associated with reading and writing. Most importantly these children perceive themselves as readers and writers and participate in these processes during the course of a normal day. Essentially it is the social and cultural practice around print that fosters understanding and enthusiasm to join in literacy events as appropriate.

Children with rich literacy backgrounds are also likely to have some knowledge of the elements of written language. They are therefore more prepared for literacy learning and are ready to make links between what they know about letters and words and what they are required to learn at school. Early success in reading and writing at school promotes further success in the later years of schooling (Crévola and Hill, 1998). Children who begin school with some awareness of print and its uses continue to show higher scores in reading and writing as they progress through their educational careers. Thus an early, but appropriate, start in literacy fosters long-term benefits for children.

Evidence of these benefits from early exposure to literacy has, however, brought further pressures on the preschool field to make greater provision for literacy. Teachers are faced with the problem of how they should approach this. Traditionally, the early childhood curriculum serves to develop the whole child within the context of language and cognition, physical development and socialisation. The preferred 'vehicle' for learning and teaching in early childhood settings is largely based on play. Teachers who regard the learning and teaching of reading and writing as being fundamentally skills-based are likely to approach early literacy instruction through formal, didactic techniques. This runs counter to the pedagogy of play and many teachers become concerned that that this will lead to the demise of play-based approaches to early education.

Pressures and problems

During our UK research observations, we have been very aware that early years practitioners in England have felt pressured by government initiatives to include more literacy in the nursery school programme. Strong political and educational pressures for a much greater emphasis on literacy appear to have been generated in response to concerns about standards in the later years of school. This concern generated a demand for more emphasis on literacy and numeracy in the nursery and in the early years of schooling. The result has been more pressure for greater emphasis on the teaching of literacy and numeracy in nurseries, from the press, politicians, parents and some powerful officials in the field of education. Evidence of this pressure can be seen in the fact that the English nursery inspection framework (Ofsted, 1998) requires the failure, or certainly a reduced period before the next inspection, of settings which do not reach required goals on provision relating to literacy and numeracy, whereas the verdict is less harsh on those who are failing to provide adequately for children's learning in the areas of creative, physical, personal and social learning, and their knowledge and understanding of the world.

This situation has created considerable tension for early childhood educators in England, particularly as it is at a time when the government is also seeking to rapidly improve the quantity of provision. Although these developments have resulted in extra funding for training, many early years educators are being expected to develop their curricula to include literacy and numeracy without the benefits of further education and training.

A consequence of this has been a piecemeal approach to change. What it has meant is that, with the best of intentions, some early years practitioners have adopted skills-based approaches to teaching reading and writing which they themselves probably experienced as children and which they may have witnessed in use with older children in primary schools.

For example, in some settings where the curriculum is being provided through free and structured play, we would see literacy activities which were adult-led, adult-directed, and separate from the other learning experiences being ably provided.

Examples of this included:

- 'workbooks' and worksheets prepared by adults – the children often appeared bored, confused, disinterested, and eager to get away, back to their friends and their play;

- activity cards with letters or words and bright pictures on them, for letter or word recognition. We saw this type of material being used in different ways, for example, we saw children being asked to find the ones which rhymed, such as 'spoon' and 'moon'. The children observed seemed to begin very eagerly, wanting to tell the adult involved what they already knew about print but gradually losing interest and deferring to the adult even when they had made sensible guesses based on what they thought the activity was about. Unfortunately, the adults would often ignore the children's suggestions which they saw as 'wrong' because they were so focused on the teaching point in their minds. These activities demanded too many language concepts at the same time and they were rarely relevant to the children's current interests and experience. The adults and children seemed to pass each other like ships in the night, because the foci of their attentions were different aspects of the materials. The adults were, with the best of intentions, trying to teach what they had planned. However, they had shifted away from their preferred child-centred approach;

- the use of a particular reading scheme with two-year-olds, which had the effect that one book-loving two-year-old simply froze when her mother showed her a story book from this phonics-based reading scheme in a local bookshop. Her usually relaxed and capable expression changed to one of utter panic. Fearing her daughter would be put off literacy for life, this mother sensibly took her child away from that particular nursery.

This shift away from child-centred teaching seems to lie in educators' lack of confidence and knowledge about early literacy learning. Their attempts at teaching more formally do make sense in the light of the National Literacy Strategy and the top-down pressure they are experiencing. The educators who adopted these methods all tried to make the experiences playful but the practice was still predicated on the notion that literacy learning is skills-based and sequential.

The assumptions the teacher brings to the teaching situation have a profound impact on the procedures adopted. Even the teachers who held a strong commitment to child-centred pedagogy have been swayed by their view of how children learn to become literate. Our experience in Australia revealed a similar confusion in the views held by teachers. Teachers were afraid that they might 'get it wrong for children'. A number of teachers were concerned for instance when they saw children beginning to write using capital letters. Teachers perceived this as 'wrong' and as such opted to leave literacy out of the curriculum rather than risk reinforcing these (wrong) responses. Again there was an inconsistency with other aspects of their teaching, since their practice was normally founded on observations of the children's play and talk, through which they could discover what individual children already knew, and plan accordingly.

Messages from research

Our central message in this book, based on our own research in four countries and drawing on research carried out by others in the field, has been about the enabling of very young children to 'make sense' of literacy in ways that 'make sense' to early years teachers.

For most of our participant educators their main concern was that their pedagogy should be appropriate for both the age group and the individual children attending their settings. We are advocating a play approach to early literacy but this does not mean there is no role for practitioners. In fact the role of early years professionals, as providers of literacy experiences for our young children, is crucial. It is a role which requires great skill and sensitivity, because this teaching must be approached through the children's concerns and interests, not through formulaic, pre-planned sessions which do not take account of children's individual knowledge bases, home cultures and present preoccupations. While the role requires meticulous planning of the setting and careful observation of children as they play, these formal aspects of the role are invisible and what is visible to the children is an environment rich in play opportunities, with adults and other children who are co-constructors of knowledge, members of a community of learners in which parents too are welcome. The ability to observe children playing and to recognise the point at which they can be helped to gain access to new knowledge by building on what they already know, and to intervene appropriately, means being knowledgeable about:

- the children engaged in that particular activity in that particular setting;

- how children learn (in different ways);

- the subject matter involved;

- the resources available to support the different learning steps each of the children will be making and how to use them.

Weaving all these threads together demands highly skilled, 'invisible pedagogy'.

In one preschool we observed this 'invisible pedagogy' in action:

Emma, Megan, Jack, Tyler, Matthew, Lucy, and Kylie have constructed a 'bus' from the large blocks. Matthew is driving. He has 'stopped' occasionally to allow his passengers to get on and now they appear to be careering through the countryside. Suddenly he shouts 'I don't know the way to Dover!' One of the female passengers says 'We need a map!' A nearby adult quietly produces a map book and hands it to the group of three- and four-year-olds. They lay it out on the floor and the adult helps them find the page with Dover on it. She explains about how maps work, what the different coloured lines mean and some of the children volunteer their knowledge about maps, who has maps at home and where they are kept. Emma suddenly says 'That's like my mum's name; she points to the town of Sandwich and the adult remembers Emma's mum is called Sandra.

> They talk about the 'Sand' syllable in Sandra and Sandwich, they recognise other letters, mostly those with which their own and other children's names begin. Then, as quickly as this episode began, the children remember their journey and are back in their places on the bus.

By engaging in 'invisible pedagogy' this practitioner was, at one and the same time, furthering the children's knowledge about literacy and forms of literacy and developing their play. The conversation was meaningful and subtly instructional.

Findings from other research projects support our own. Following their work involving practitioners from different types of settings, Angela Anning and Anne Edwards (1999: 102-5) provide detailed lists of early language and literacy behaviours in children from birth to five and alongside these they placed 'what adults can do'. Linda Miller (1996) suggests adults in preschool settings should adopt a role more like that of adults at home, with all the warmth and closeness involved. In her later work (Miller, 2000), she cites Guy Claxton's 'slow ways of knowing', and his contention that early years teachers need to attend to this if we are to avoid damaging children through 'the sausage machine of literacy'. Meanwhile Jeni Riley provides evidence that children who read and write early have one thing in common: 'they are knowledgeable about and understand the communicative function of the written word' (1996:26).

Similarly, research by Kathy Sylva et al. (1999, 1999a) suggests that a 'focused literacy programme', where teachers have attended inservice sessions (including watching another teacher model a range of strategies and information about early literacy research and about planning print-rich classrooms), is more successful than a relatively narrow and less relevant programme focusing on exercises and direct instruction. Further, the children involved in the 'focused literacy' programme achieved higher results on literacy tests, despite the fact that they spent roughly the same amount of time on literacy in both types of classes.

According to Penny Munn (1994), practitioners need to understand what early literacy activities mean to the children themselves, since her research demonstrated that the adults' and children's interpretations of experiences involving print were different.

In reporting on her research conversations with four-year-olds, Jacqui Cousins tells of children's accounts of their favourite stories and of their offers to 'read you a story'. While they did so, Cousins was able to watch

> how well the children pointed to the words, followed the print left to right, recognised letters of their names and turned the pages...All that awareness of print pointed to their understanding of the reading process...in every case the families said the children had 'caught' reading rather than being 'taught' by them. Cousins (1999:50-1)

When observing settings in which there was little understanding of the potential role of play for literacy and numeracy development, Jacqui Cousins found that play areas which were accessible to the children but unattended by an adult often resulted in 'time-wasting and chaotic' activities in 'a frightening space' (p.55). As with our own research, Cousins found that 'many adults were doing a magnificent job but needed more training' so that they could use information from research about children's development and learning through play in *all* areas of the curriculum, including literacy and numeracy (p.56).

Summing up, Marion Whitehead (1999:119-21) argues that there are four essential, humane strategies to her

- 24-hour literacy' programme:
- talk, play and representation;
- rhyme, rhythm and language patterns;
- stories and narratives;
- environmental print and messages.

Further support for play approaches to early learning is also evident in the new *Early Learning Goals* (QCA, 1999, 2000) to be adopted in settings for children aged from three to five years in England from September 2000, following extensive consultations with practitioners and experts in the field.

The commonalities in the different projects and our own lie in:

- the range of literacy opportunities for which practitioners need to plan imaginatively, with the children in their own settings in mind;

- formality 'in the heads' of the practitioners (and in their planning), not in using instructional activities initiated and directed by them (the teachers). So practitioners themselves need to be informed about play, literacy (how it 'works', what it is 'for'), as well as being informed about research on early literacy, theories of child development and learning, observation techniques and how notes from observations inform planning and practice. They engage in a synthesis of theory and practice – known as 'praxis';

- the 'modelling' of literacy behaviours and language by practitioners;

- capitalising on 'teachable moments' and 'literacy events' (tailored to the children's preoccupations);

- 'invisible' pedagogy, promoting learning through play.

A way ahead

In our four-country research we found that many children were engaging in literate behaviour in their own free-choice activities but not all the teachers set out to foster development of literacy for the children, that opportunities for 'making sense' through relevant play approaches to literacy were often limited and that many feared the loss of play-based approaches.

One of the outcomes of the projects has been the ease with which literacy can be developed in the early years curriculum, and there are examples of this in Chapters 6 and 7.

Some teachers were already providing excellent play-based opportunities for their children to engage in early literacy encounters. When those teachers who felt anxious about the introduction of literacy into the early years curriculum were given professional support they were more confident to examine the issues of literacy in their curricula. They were able to set their own goals and explore ways of engaging in literacy that were consistent with a child-focused pedagogy. A move towards literacy provision in preschool does not mean that established child-centred approaches should be replaced by more formal instruction but that children should be supported to pursue their own interests through invisible pedagogy. Above all, the issue in literacy education and the early years is not whether it should be included or excluded. Rather, the issue is how do we include it to ensure that all children have the benefit of becoming legitimate members of a print-dependent society. The knowledge and attitudes children form during their early years will have a lasting impact on their later success.

There needs to be a greater understanding of the importance of early experience in children's interest and motivation towards literacy. The early childhood field needs to embrace a view of literacy which acknowledges it as a social as well as a cognitive phenomenon. A great deal of evidence is available today that supports a socially constructed view of literacy development in addition to a cognitive view. Literacy learning involves attitudes and motivations along with knowledge and skills. Children learn literacy practices in partnerships with others around them who use literacy. Children need models of literate practice to gain insights into this social convention. Parents and teachers who avoid literacy with young children put them at risk and prevent them from developing a social awareness about print and its many uses. Furthermore, on arriving at school, children with limited literacy experiences will be disadvantaged because they will not have the necessary insight into what they should learn or why. Thus early childhood practitioners have a responsibility for ensuring that all children begin schooling with a 'good start', a good start built on understandings about what is culturally relevant as well as elemental knowledge. In this book we have shown that literacy can be introduced in ways that are in harmony with play-based approaches to early teaching and learning.

We have also argued that children have the right to be empowered members of their own communities and of society at large. We are faced with new insights into our responsibilities as early childhood practitioners. Current knowledge and understanding about the early childhood years and the impact of experience on children's long-term success (or otherwise) help us to appreciate the early years curriculum as part of the whole sphere of influence over children's development.

Children benefit when there is continuity in their experience. The role of the early childhood setting is to create links with what children bring with them from home and to provide a foundation for the understandings they need to take with them to school. But one of its key roles is to enable children to participate fully in their worlds here and now.

Early years teachers who recognise that the approaches they adopt to foster young children's understanding of literacy can be embedded in a curriculum based on play provide subtle 'instruction' through careful planning, observing and intervening with suggestions, support and the use of 'teachable moments'. Such teachers are 'formal in their heads' – they know what children are trying to learn by observing them, they know what the next step will be for a particular child and they provide for it in ways that 'make sense' to that child. They adopt an 'invisible' pedagogy to ensure that children engage in literacy events and then they capitalise on the teachable moments. Above all they convey to children the enjoyment that can be found in both reading and writing, the different forms these can take, the different media that can be used to express ideas and views.

The Australian research two years on

Children in the Australian project were followed up during their first two years in school. They entered primary schools along with children from other centres who had not been involved in the project. The total number of children in this cohort was approximately 1000, with more than 300 having attended the project centres. Project and non-project children were assessed on a number of measures at the time they started school and subsequently at the end of their first and their second years in school.

After one year in school, the project children were reading on average three 'text levels' ahead of the non-project children, an advantage that was maintained over their second year in school. Interestingly, on entry to school, the project children were indistinguishable from the non-project children when asked to read from a school level text, as might be expected. None of the children could read as no-one had explicitly taught them to do that. However, on entry to school, the project children had more concepts about print, scored higher on a test of oral language, could write more words in ten minutes, read more high frequency words from a list of 15 and could make more accurate marks to a dictated sentence (Raban: in press).

When these data were interrogated for the influence of age and gender, the results did not change. What we are seeing here is the project children arriving in school with greater understandings of the purposes and functions of print, and a greater insight into the nature of literate activity. They have gained this from the enriched environment of the preschool programme and from the many experiences of interactions involving print. This gave them foundational understandings through which they could benefit more rapidly from the explicit teaching of reading and writing that they encountered on entry to school, an advantage they have been able to maintain.

When children arrive in school and respond positively to a teaching pro- gramme, the feedback they experience in terms of their successfully developing skills and their ability to benefit more widely from their schooling provides powerful reinforcement.

Babies and literacy

In our projects we have focused mainly on children aged between three and five or six years old, but we endorse the idea that children in print- dependent societies are learning about literacy from their earliest days. It is likely that many societies have underestimated the power of babies to 'make sense' of their worlds too. By observing them and by listening to those with whom they are most familiar, we can learn much that will astonish us about their early capabilities.

The 1997 exhibition from the nurseries of Reggio Emilia showed four photographs of eight-month-old Laura with her nursery worker looking at a page of watches in a catalogue. In the third picture Laura is listening to the tick of the worker's wrist-watch, and in the last of the photographs, Laura has put her ear to the page of watches – to test if they too are ticking. Laura has 'read' the page of symbols and is hypothesising about the similarity and difference between these and the worker's watch.

Although we have not included them here, we have experienced numerous instances of babies making sense of pictures in books, enjoy- ing photograph albums of people they know well, revelling in videos of favourite picture books – such as *The very hungry caterpillar,* whose burps and gurgling stomach cause much merriment to nine-month-olds like Kieran. As we argued in Chapter 2, the potential for rapid brain development between birth and three, and the natural curiosity to know about and make sense of their worlds with which babies are born, mean that the best advice we can give to parents is to enjoy conversations and relaxed, happy experiences with their children. Research and development work such as that by Cathy Nutbrown and Peter Hannon (1997) is particularly informative for practitioners seeking to engage parents in sharing their children's early literacy experiences.

Learning communities

Perhaps what has come through most strongly from our projects is the eagerness of so many of our participants to share in discussion about ways that really do make sense of teaching young children about literacy. We have also been impressed by the desire for more knowledge among those practitioners who feel less confident about their role in developing children's early literacy and their willingness to give their own time to this development. If we begin to regard early childhood settings as centres of lifelong learning for children, parents, teachers and local communities, where knowledge is shared and time for reading is prioritised, then reflection and discussion are seen as essential.

Learning communities can be formed in many different ways, especially now with the advent of e-mail. Local collaboration is clearly the first layer of such communities.

One important aspect of the local versions of these learning communities would be the links and sharing of knowledge between preschool and primary teachers. Such links are vital if children are to experience greater continuity in their experience and in order that there is mutual understanding about practice. Primary school teachers would benefit if all the children from a local preschool, where children had been helped to 'make sense' of a print-rich context, came to them with some understanding of literacy and 'how print works' – the benefit being a narrower gap between the most and least able children vis-à-vis literacy.

An excellent example of such a learning community is the Billericay Early Years Forum in England. Early years practitioners in this area of Essex came together to produce their own guidelines for local early childhood educators – *Building Foundations for Literacy* (Billericay Early Years Forum, 1999). Similarly, in Australia, a collection of ideas for practice linking sessional preschool, childcare settings and family involvement, has been prepared by early years professionals who have addressed *Issues and Practices in Literacy Development* (AECA, 1999).

By networking, and sharing ideas and practice across boundaries, we learn about ourselves, for we are constantly challenged by the way others in different settings, or countries, 'see' the world and young children. We begin to question the constructions of childhood we have taken for granted, and the limits we may have put upon young children's opportunities to make sense of their worlds. We may also begin to question whether we have limited children's access to 'the hundred languages' of which they are capable – different forms of expression, from art, poetry, music, movement and dance, to computer graphics, mathematics, mechanics, sculpture and 3-D modelling, in which print literacy forms only a part, connected with and often embedded within those others symbolic systems.

As members of the research teams, we too have been crossing boundaries, between countries, cultures, languages, disciplines, research backgrounds, and each others' assumptions and understandings. The 'journeys' have been exhilarating, challenging and full of debate, because the field is complex and there is still much to explore.

Above all we have been privileged to spend time with dedicated practitioners, and the children and parents with whom they work, in four countries. The boundaries between research, theory and practice have been blurred as we have all been amazed by young children's capabilities as they have engaged in literacy learning, and together we have sought the most appropriate ways to teach them – to help them 'make sense' of literacy.

Endnote to illustrate literacy as social practice, developed through experience rather than didactic instruction during the preschool years:

> Coralie, Tricia's granddaughter (aged four) had asked what her 'Nana' does when she goes to a nursery. Tricia had explained that she writes down what the children are doing, but she did not explain anything further, nor was she asked to at that point. One day as Coralie's mother, Sacha, was driving her to her nursery, the following conversation ensued:
>
> C: I think Nana's going to nursery today.
>
> S: Mmm, I'm not sure... What does she do when she goes to a nursery?
>
> C: She writes down what the children are doing – it's for her work.
>
> S: Oh and what does she do after that?
>
> C: She prints it out – so other people can read it.

Bibliography

AECA (1999) *Issues and Practices in Literacy Development.* Canberra, ACT: Australian Early Childhood Association Inc.

Anning, A. and Edwards, A. (1999) *Promoting Children's Learning from Birth to Five: developing the new early years professional.* Buckingham: Open University Press

Auzias, M. and de Ajuraguerria, J. (1986) Les fonctions culturelles de l'écriture et les conditions de son développement chez l'enfant. *Enfance* nos 2–3, pp.145-67

Barratt-Pugh, C. (1997) 'Why d'you speak funny?' – supporting all children learning to talk and talking to learn. In L.Abbott and H. Moylett (eds) *Working with the Under-3s: responding to children's needs.* Buckingham: Open University Press. pp.75-89

Barrière, I. (forthcoming) Developmental psycholinguistics: contributions to understanding children's languages and minds. In T.David (ed.) *Applied Research in Early Childhood Education.* London: JAI Publishing Limited

Barrière, I. Jago, M. and Goouch, K. (1999) L'éveil à la lecture et à l'écriture en France. *International Journal of Early Childhood* vol.31(2) pp.65-74

Barton, D. (1994) *Literacy: an introduction to the ecology of written language.* Blackwell: Oxford

Béchennec, D. and Sprenger-Charolles, L. (1997) Literacy Teaching in France in V. Edwards and D. Corson. (eds) *Encyclopedia of Language and Education. vol. 2: Literacy.* The Netherlands: Kluwer Academic Press. pp191-8.

Bennett, N., Wood, L. and Rogers, S. (1997) *Teaching through Play.* Buckingham: Open University Press

Billericay Early Years Forum (1999) *Fun With Literacy.* Billericay: Billericay Early Years Forum

Bissex, G. (1980) *Gyns at Wrk: A child learns to read and write.* Cambridge, Massachusetts: Harvard University Press

Blanche-Beneveniste, C., Pallaud, B. and Hennequin, M.L. (1992) *Rapports: enfants de Romans: les performances langagières d'enfants francophones et non francophones d'origine, dans des classes de grande section maternelle.* Marseilles: Université de Provence Aix

Bochner, S., Price, P. and Jones, J. (1997) *Child Language Development: learning to talk.* London: Whurr Books

Britton, J. (1970) *Language and Learning.* Harmondsworth: Pelican

Bronfenbrenner, U. (1979) *The Ecology of Human Development: experiments by nature and design.* Cambridge, Massachusetts: Harvard University Press

Bronfenbrenner, U. and Morris, P. (1998) The ecology of developmental processes. In W.Damon (ed.) *The Handbook of Child Psychology Vol.1 Theoretical Models of Human Development.* New York: John Wiley

Brooks, G., Schagen, I., Nastat, P., Lilly, J., Papadopolou, C. and Othman, Y. (1997) *Trends in Reading at Eight.* Slough: NFER

Bruce, T. (1991) *Time to Play in Early Childhood Education.* London: Hodder and Stoughton

Bruner, J. (1986) *Actual Minds, Possible Worlds.* Cambridge, Massachusetts: Harvard University Press

Bruner, J.S. (1960) *The Process of Education.* Cambridge, Massachusetts: Harvard University Press

Cairney, T. (1995) *Pathways to Literacy.* London: Cassell

Campbell, R. (1996) *Literacy in nursery education.* Stoke-on-Trent: Trentham Books

Campbell, R. (1998) A three year old learning literacy at home. *Early Years* vol. 19 (1) pp.76-89

Campbell, R. (1999) *Literacy from Home to School: reading with Alice.* Stoke-on-Trent: Trentham Books

Carle, E. (1969) *The Very Hungry Caterpillar.* London: Hamish Hamilton

Carle, E. (1982) *The Bad-tempered Ladybird.* Harmondsworth: Penguin/Picture Puffins

Carter, D (2000) *Teaching Fiction in the Primary School.* London: David Fulton

Chartier, A. M., Clesse, C. and Hébrard, J. (1997) *Lire écrire: entrer dans le monde de l'écrit au Cycle 2.* Paris: Hatier

Chauveau, G., Rémond, M. and Rogovas-Chauveau, E. (1993) *L'enfant apprenti lecteur: l'entrée dans le système de l'écrit.* Collection CRESAS, No.10. Paris: INRP / l'Harmattan

Chukovsky, K. (1963) *From Two to Five.* Berkeley: University of California Press

Clark, L. (2000) Lessons from the nursery: children as writers in early education. *Reading* vol.34 (2) pp.69-74

Clay, M.M. (1969) Reading errors and self-correction behaviour. *British Journal of Educational Psychology* vol.39 pp. 47–56

Clay, M.M. (1975) *What Did I Write?* Auckland, NZ: Heinemann

Clay, M.M. (1998) *By Different Paths to Common Outcomes.* Yorke, Maine: Stenhouse

Coffield, F (1997) A tale of three little pigs: building the learning society with straw. In F.Coffield (ed.) *A National Strategy for Lifelong Learning.* Newcastle-upon-Tyne: University of Newcastle. pp.77-93

Cousins, J. (1999) *Listening to Four Year Olds.* London: NEYN

Crévola, C. and Hill, P. (1998) Initial evaluation of a whole school approach to prevention and intervention in early literacy. *Journal of Education for Children Placed at Risk* vol.3 (2) pp.133-57

David, T. (1990) *Under Five, Under-educated?* Milton Keynes: Open University Press

David, T. (ed.) (1993) *Educating our Youngest Children: European Perspectives.* London: PCP

David, T. (ed.) (1998) *Researching Early Childhood Education: European Perspectives.* London: PCP

David, T. (ed.) (1999) *Teaching Young Children.* London: PCP/Sage

David, T. (1999a) *Second Interim of the ELL-Early Literacy Links Project. Submitted to the Esmée Fairbairn Charitable Trust.* Canterbury: Centre for Educational Research, CCCUC

David, T., Barrière, I., Jago, M. and Goouch, K. (1999) *The Early Literacy Links Project (ELL Project) Interim Report.* Submitted to the Esmée Fairbairn Charitable Trust. Canterbury: Centre for Educational Research, CCCUC

David, T. and Nurse, A. (1999) Inspections of under fives' education and constructions of childhood. In T.David (ed.) *Teaching Young Children.* London: PCP/Sage. pp.165-84

DfEE (1998) *The National Literacy Strategy.* London: DfEE

DfEE (1999) *The National Numeracy Strategy.* London: DfEE

DfEE (1999a) *Tomorrow's Children: the review of pre-schools and playgroups and the Government's response.* London: DfEE

Docking, J. (ed.) (2000) *New Labour's Policies for Schools: raising the standard?* London: David Fulton

Dombey, H. (1998) Changing Literacy in the Early Years. In B. Cox (ed.) *Literacy is Not Enough.* Manchester: Book Trust. pp.125-32

Downing, J. and Fijalkow, J. (1984) *Lire et raisonner.* Toulouse: Privat

Edwards, C., Gandini, L. and Foreman, G. (1998) *The Hundred Languages of Children: the Reggio Emilia approach – advanced reflections.* London: Ablex

Edwards, D. and Mercer, N. (1987) *Common Knowledge.* London: Methuen

Einarsdottir, J. (1996) Dramatic play and print. *Childhood Education* vol.72(6) pp. 352–57

Fayol , M. (1997) Preface to Chartier, Clesse and Hébrard (1997) (q.v.)

Ferreiro, E. and Teborosky, A. (1983) *Literacy Before Schooling.* London: Heinemann.

Fijalkow, J. (1997) *Entrer dans l'écrit.* Tournai: Magnard.

Garcia-Debanc, C., Grandaty, M. and Liva, A. (eds) (1996) *Didactique de la lecture: regards croisés.* Toulouse: Presses Universitaires du Mirail

Gardner, H. (1991) *The Unschooled Mind: how children think and how schools should teach.* London: Fontana

Geekie, P., Cambourne, B. and Fitzsimmons, P. (1999) *Understanding Literacy Development.* Stoke-on-Trent: Trentham Books

Goodman, K.S. (1967) Reading: a psycholinguistic guessing game. *Journal of the Reading Specialist* vol. 4 pp.126–35.

Goodman, Y. (1986) Children coming to know literacy. In W. Teale and J. Sulzby (eds) *Emergent Literacy: reading and writing.* Norwood, New Jersey: Ablex

Gopnik, A., Meltzoff, A. and Kuhl, P. (1999) *How Babies Think.* London: Weidenfield and Nicolson

Goutard, M. (1993) Preschool education in France in T.David (ed.) *Educating our Youngest Children: European perspectives.* London: PCP. pp.35-55

Graham, J. (1999) The creation of readers or Mr Magnolia meets the Literacy Hour. Will he survive? In P.Goodwin *The Literate Classroom.* London: David Fulton. pp.65-71

Grainger, T. and Goouch, K. (1999) Young children and playful language. In T.David (ed) *Teaching Young Children*. London: PCP/Sage. pp.19-29

Grainger, T. and Lambirth, A (1999) *Poetry: voice and body Paper given at a conference of the International Federation of Teachers of English*. Warwick University. Coventry, July 1999

Graves, D. (1983) *Writing: teachers and children at work*. London: Heinemann

Gregory, E. and Biarnès, J. (1994) Tony and Jean-François looking for sense in the strangeness of school. In H. Dombey and M. Meek Spencer (eds) *First Steps Together*. Stoke-on-Trent: Trentham Books. pp.15-30

Gregory, E. (1996) *Making Sense of a New World*. London: PCP

Gregory, E. (ed) (1997) *One Child, Many Worlds: early learning in multicultural communities*. London: David Fulton

Hall, B. (1997) *Madeleine's world: a biography of a three-year-old*. London: Vintage

Hall, L. (1989) *A Practical Guide to Teaching Poetry in the Primary Classroom*. London: Cassell

Hall, N. (1987) *The Emergence of Literacy*. Sevenoaks, Kent: Hodder and Stoughton

Hall, N. and Robinson, A. (1995) *Exploring Writing and Play in the Early Years*. London: David Fulton

Hamers, J. and Blanc, M.H.A. (2000) *Bilinguality and Bilingualism*. Cambridge: CUP

Hébrard, J. (1988) Apprendre à lire à l'école en France: un siècle de recommandations officielles. *Langue Française* no. 80, pp.111-28

Hendricks, H. (1997) Constructions and reconstructions of British childhood: an interpretative survey, 1800 to the present. In A. James and A. Prout (eds) *Constructing and Reconstructing Childhood*. London: Falmer Press. pp. 19-34

Higonnet, A. (1998) *Pictures of Innocence: the history and crisis of ideal childhood*. London: Thames and Hudson

Hillman, M., Adams, J. and Whitelegg, J. (1990) *One False Move ... a study of children's independent mobility*. London: Policy Studies Institute

Hilton, M. (ed.) (1996) *Potent Fictions*. London: Routledge

Hilton, M. (1998) Raising reading standards: the true story. *English in Education*. vol. 32 (3) pp.4–16

HMI (1978) *Primary Education in England: a survey by Her Majesty's Inspectors of Schools*. London: HMSO

Hunt, J.McV. (1961) *Intelligence and Experience*. New York: Ronald

Hurry, J., Sylva, K. and Riley, J. (1999) Evaluation of a focused literacy teaching programme in Reception and Year 1 classes: child outcomes. *British Education Research Journal* vol.25 (5) pp.637-50

Jago, M. (1999) Bilingual children in a monolingual society. In David, T (ed.) *Young Children Learning*. London: Paul Chapman. pp.156-67

Jago, M. (2000) Foreign Languages in Early Schooling: policy, pupils and processes. Unpublished doctoral thesis, University of Kent at Canterbury.

James, A. and Prout, A. (eds) (1997) *Constructing and reconstructing childhood. 2nd edition*. London: Falmer Press

Kantor, R., Miller, S. and Fernie, D. (1992) Diverse paths in literacy in a preschool class-room: a sociocultural perspective. *Reading Research Quarterly.* vol.27 pp.185–201.

Katz, L. and Chard, S.C. (1988) *Engaging Children's Minds: the project approach.* Norwood, New Jersey: Ablex.

Kress, G. (1982) *Learning to Write.* London: Routledge

Kress, G. (1997) *Before Writing: rethinking the paths to literacy.* London: Routledge

Kress, G. (2000) *Early Spelling.* London: Routledge

Lindsay, G. (2000) Researching children's perspectives: ethical issues. In A. Lewis and G. Lindsay (eds) *Researching Children's Perspectives.* Buckingham: Open University Press pp.3–20

Mayall, B. (1996) *Children, Health and the Social Order.* Buckingham: Open University Press.

MCEETYA (1999) *The Adelaide Declaration: the national goals for schooling in the twenty-first century.* Canberra, ACT: Commonwealth of Australia

McLane, J. and McNamee, G. (1990) *Early Literacy.* Cambridge, Massachusetts: Harvard University Press

Meade, A. (forthcoming) One hundred billion neurons: how do they become organised? In T.David (ed.) *Applied Research in Early Childhood Education.* London: JAI Publishing Ltd.

Meadows, S. (1993) *The Child as Thinker.* London: Routledge

Medwell, J., Wray, D., Poulson, L. and Fox, R. (1998) *Effective Teachers of Literacy.* Exeter: University of Exeter

Meek, M. (1991) *On Being Literate.* London: Bodley Head

Meek, M. (1998) Important reading lessons. In B.Cox (ed.) *Literacy is Not Enough.* Manchester: Book Trust. pp.116–24

Miller, A. (1987) *For Your Own Good: hidden cruelty in child rearing and the roots of violence.* London: Virago

Miller, L. (1996) *Towards Reading.* Buckingham: Open University Press

Miller, L. (2000) Play as a foundation for learning. In R.Drury, L.Miller and R.Campbell (eds) *Looking at Early Years Education and Care.* London: David Fulton

Mills, C. (1998) Britain's early years disaster. Paper for Channel 4 Television programme 'Too Much Too Soon'. London: Channel 4

Ministère de l'Éducation Nationale (1991) *Les cycles à l'école primaire.* Paris: CNDP-Hachette

Ministère de l'Éducation Nationale (1992) *La maîtrise de la langue à l'école.* Paris: CNDP-Savoir Livre

Ministère de l'Éducation Nationale, de la Recherche et de la Technologie (1998) *Géographie de 'école.* Paris: Direction de la programmation et du développement

Minns, H. (1990) *Read It To Me Now!* London: Virago/ London University Institute of Education

Morrow, L.M. (1990) Preparing the classroom environment to promote literacy during play. *Early Childhood Research Quarterly.* vol.5 (4) pp.537–54.

Morrow, L.M. (1991) Relationships among physical design of play centres, and children's literacy behaviours during play. In J. Zutell and S. McCormick (Eds.) *Learner Factors/Teacher Factors: issues in literacy research and instruction.* 40th Yearbook of the National Reading Conference. National Reading Conference: Chicago. pp. 127–40

Morrow, L.M. and Rand, M. (1991) Promoting literacy during play by designing early childhood classroom environments. *The Reading Teacher* vol. 44 pp.396–402.

Morss, J. (1990) *The Biologizing of Childhood.* London: Routledge

Munn, P. (1994) The early development of literacy and numeracy skills. *European Early Childhood Education Research Journal* vol.2 (1) pp.5-18

Nelson, K. (1986) *Event Knowledge: structure and function in development.* Hillsdale, New Jersey: Erlbaum

Neuman, S. and Roskos, K. (1991) The influence of literacy-enriched play centres on preschoolers' conceptions of the functions of print. In J.Christie (ed.) *Play and Early Literacy Development.* Albany: State University of New York Press pp. 167–87

Neuman, S. and Roskos, K. (1997) Literacy knowledge in practice: contexts of participation for young writers and readers. *Reading Research Quarterly.* Vol.32 pp.10–32

Nutbrown, C. (1997) *Recognising Early Literacy Development: assessing children's achievements.* London: Paul Chapman.

Nutbrown, C. (1998) *The Lore and Language of Early Education.* Sheffield: Sheffield University Division of Education

Nutbrown, C. (1999) *Threads of thinking. 2nd edition.* London: Paul Chapman.

Nutbrown, C. and Hannon, P. (eds) (1997) *Preparing for Early Literacy Education with Parents.* Nottingham: NES Arnold

Oberhuemer, P. and Ulich, M. (1997) *Working with Young Children in Europe: provision and staff training.* London: Paul Chapman

Ofsted (1998) *Guidance on the Inspection of Nursery Education Provision in the Private, Voluntary and Independent Sectors.* London: OFSTED

Ofsted (1999) *The Quality of Nursery Education.* London: OFSTED

Olson, D. (1994) *The World on Paper.* Cambridge: Cambridge University Press.

Olson, D. (1998) There are x kinds of learners in a single class: diversity without individual differences. In J.S. Gaffney and B.J. Askew (eds) *Stirring the Waters: the influence of Marie Clay.* Portsmouth, New Hampshire: Heinemann.

Ozga, J. (2000) *Policy Research in Educational Settings: contested terrain.* Buckingham: Open University Press

Panter-Brick, C.(ed.) (1997) *Biological Perspectives on Childhood.* Cambridge: Cambridge University Press

Piaget, J. (1955) *The Child's Construction of Reality.* London: Routledge and Kegan Paul.

Pickett, L. (1998) Literacy learning during block play. *Journal of Research in Childhood Education* vol.12 (2) pp. 225-30

QCA (1999) *Early Learning Goals.* London: QCA/DfEE

QCA (2000) *A Curriculum Framework for the Foundation Stage.* London: QCA/ DfEE

Raban, B. (in press) *Just the Beginning...Department of Education, Training and Youth affairs Research Fellowship Report No.1.* Canberra ACT: Commonwealth of Australia

Raban, B. and Ure, C. (1999) Literacy in three languages: a challenge for Singaporean preschools. *International Journal of Early Childhood* vol.31(2) pp.45-54

Raban, B. and Ure, C. (2000) Literacy in the preschool: an Australian case-study. In J. Hayden (ed.) *Landscapes in Early Childhood Education: cross-national perspectives on empowerment – a guide for the new millennium.* New York: Peter Lang. pp.375-90

Reeves, J. (1965) *The Cassell Book of English Poetry.* London: Cassell

Reynolds, B. (1997) *Literacy in the Preschool: the roles of teachers and parents.* Stoke-on-Trent: Trentham Books

Rieben, L. and Perfetti, C. (eds) (1989) *L'appenti-lecteur: recherches empiriques et implications pédagogiques.* Neuchatel: Delachaux et Niestlé.

Riley, J. (1996) *The Teaching of Reading.* London: PCP

Riley, J. (1999) *Teaching Reading.* London: Stanley Thornes

Rosen, M. (1989) *Did I Hear You Write.* Nottingham: Five Leaves

Rosen, M. and Barrs, M. (1997) *A Year With Poetry.* London: CLPE

Roskos, K. and Neuman, S. (1993) Descriptive observations of adults' facilitation of literacy in young children's play. *Early Childhood Research Quarterly.* vol.8 pp.77–97.

Rowe, D.W. (1998) The literate potentials of book-related dramatic play. *International Reading Research Quarterly.* vol.33 pp.10–35

SCAA (1996) *Desirable Outcomes for Children's Learning.* London: SCAA/DfEE

Schrader, C. (1991) Symbolic play: a source of meaningful engagement with writing and reading. In J. Christie (ed.) *Play and Early Literacy Development.* Albany: State University of New York Press. pp. 189–213

Sedgewick, F (1997) *Read My Mind.* Routledge: London

Shorrocks, D. (1992) Evaluating Key Stage 1 assessments. *Early Years.* vol.13 pp.16-20

Smith, F (1978) *Reading.* Cambridge: Cambridge University Press

Sprenger-Charolles (1988) Présentation. In L. Sprenger-Charolles and J. David (eds) *Langue Française: la lecture et son apprentissage* (Special Issue) No.80 pp.3–5

Strandell, H. (2000) What is the use of children's play: preparation or social participation? In H. Penn (ed.) *Early Childhood Services: theory, policy and practice.* Buckingham: Open University Press

Suschitzky, W. and Chapman, J. (1998) *Valued Children, Informed Teaching.* Buckingham: Open University Press

Sylva, K., Siraj-Blatchford, I. and Johnson, S. (1992) The impact of the UK National Curriculum on pre-school practice. *International Journal of Early Childhood* Vol.24 (1) pp.41-51

Sylva, K., Hurry, J., Mirelman, H. Burrell, A. and Riley, J. (1999) Evaluation of a focused literacy teaching programme in Reception and Year 1 classes: classroom observations. *British Education Research Journal* Vol.25 (5) pp.617-636

Tabouret-Keller, A., Le Page, R.B., Gardner-Chloros, P. and Varro, G. (1997) *Vernacular Literacy*. Oxford: OUP

Taylor, D. (1983) *Family Literacy: young children learning to read and write.* Portsmouth, New Hampshire: Heinemann

Teale, W.H. and Martinez, M.G. (1989) Fostering emergent literacy in kindergarten children. In J. Mason (ed.) *Reading and Writing Connections*. Boston: Allyn and Bacon pp. 177–198

Tizard, B. and Hughes, M. (1984) *Young Children Learning*. London: Fontana

Tobin, J.J., Wu, D.Y.H. and Davidson, D.H. (1989) *Preschool in Three Cultures: Japan, China and the United States.* London: Yale University Press

Trevarthen, C. (1992) An infant's motives for speaking and thinking in the culture. In A.H. Wold (ed.) *The Dialogical Alternative.* Oxford: Oxford University Press. pp.99–137

United Nations (1959) *The Declaration on the Rights of the Child.* New York: UN

United Nations (1989) *The Convention on the Rights of the Child.* New York: UN

Van der Eyken, W. (ed.) (1975) *Education, the Child and Society: a documentary history, 1900-1973.* Harmondsworth: Penguin

Vygotsky, L.S. (1978) *Mind and Society: the development of higher psychological processes.* New York: MIT Press

Vygotsky, L.S. (1986) *Thought and Language.* New York: MIT Press

Walker, C.A., Allen, D. and Glines, D. (1997) Should we travel by plane, car, train or bus? Teacher/child collaboration in developing a thematic literacy centre. *Reading Teacher* vol.50 (6) pp. 524–27

Weinberger, J. (1996) *Literacy Goes to School.* London: PCP

Wells, G. (1986) *The Meaning Makers*. Portsmouth, New Hampshire: Heinemann

Westbrook, J. (1999) Two points of view: young children's literacy development in print and the audio visual image. *International Journal of Early Childhood* vol.31(2) pp.37-44

Whitehead, M. R. (1997) *Language and Literacy in the Early Years. 2nd edition.* London: Paul Chapman

Whitehead, M. R. (1999) A literacy hour in the nursery? The Big Question Mark. *Early Years* vol.19 (2) pp. 38-61

Whitehead, M. R. (1999a) *Supporting Language and Literacy Development in the Early Years.* Buckingham: Open University Press

Wood, D. (1988) *How Children Think and Learn.* Oxford: Basil Blackwell

Wood, E. and Attfield, J. (1996) *Play, Learning and the Early Childhood Curriculum.* London: PCP

Yaden, D.B., Rowe, D.W. and MacGillivray, L. (1999) *Emergent literacy: a polyphony of perspectives. CIERA Report no. 1-005*, University of Michigan: Ann Arbor.

INDEX